Disclaimer

Every effort has been made to ensure that the information contained within this guide is accurate at the time of publication. How2become Ltd are not responsible for anyone failing any part of any selection process as a result of the information contained within this guide. How2become Ltd and their authors cannot accept any responsibility for any errors or omissions within this guide, however caused. No responsibility for loss or damage occasioned by any person acting, or refraining from action, as a result of the material in this publication can be accepted by How2become Ltd.

The information within this guide does not represent the views of any third party service or organisation.

CONTENTS

how2become

HOW TO BECOME
A SOCIAL WORKER

Bury College
Millennium LRC

www.How2Become.com

Orders: Please contact How2become Ltd, Suite 2, 50 Churchill Square Business Centre, Kings Hill, Kent ME19 4YU.

You can order through Amazon.co.uk under ISBN 978-1-910602-29-4, via the website www.How2Become.com or through Gardners.com.

ISBN: 978-1-910602-29-4

First published in 2015 by How2become Ltd.

Typeset for How2become Ltd by Anton Pshinka.

Printed in Great Britain for How2become Ltd by:
CMP (uk) Limited, Poole, Dorset.

INTRODUCTION

How to become a Social Worker

Welcome to How2Become: The ultimate guide to becoming a social worker. This book has been designed to help you reach your dream job. We hope you find it useful, and wish you the very best of luck with your career aspirations.

On the 17th March every year, the world celebrates Social Work Day. This is an international celebration of the combined efforts of the planet's leading social work organisations: The International Federation of Social Workers, The International Association of Schools of Social Work, and The International Council of Social Welfare. Together, these three organisations are responsible for influencing international, regional and local policies, and highlighting the everyday contributions and values of social workers throughout the world.

In many places, social workers have an unfair reputation. Blamed when events go wrong, and ignored when they go right; the reputation of social work has suffered as a result of reduced budgets and overworked employees. Media outlets regularly lace their headlines with words such as 'incompetent', 'lazy' and 'irresponsible'. Parents see social workers as untrustworthy, or act as if they have come to take their children away. The reality is quite the opposite. Social workers do everything in their power to keep families together. The hard work that employees so frequently put into the role is undercut by an uncaring system, and budget restraints. Social workers can make a huge difference, which often goes unnoticed by those on the outside looking in. As a social worker, you have a fantastic opportunity to change people's lives for the better. In times of economic and social difficulty, it is social workers who are responsible for helping people to cope with changes and produce a positive contribution to society. It is social workers who help people to deal with issues such as mental health, family breakdown, bereavement and physical illness. In the current climate, social workers are more important than ever before. If you are someone who loves to help people and change their lives for the better, this could be the perfect role for you.

Before you read any further, it is important that we establish a common misconception. The terms 'social work' and 'social care work' are often used interchangeably. However, they are not the same. 'Social care work' is a term which refers to all of the social services provided to individuals in need. The term 'social work', on the other hand, refers to a specialist role within the social sector that focuses on dealing with specific individuals or groups of people who require safeguarding services. Social workers have more responsibility, qualifications and legal protection than social care workers, and are generally tasked with supervising the latter. In this guide, we will focus specifically on social workers.

This book has been broken down into useful sections, to help you gain a better understanding of the process involved. Written in conjunction with trained professionals, our How2become team have done their utmost to provide you with an in-depth guide that will assist your journey to become a social worker. We will show you which courses to take at GCSE and A Level, how to navigate your undergraduate and postgraduate degrees, where to find work experience, and how to become successful within the field of social work. We will fully prepare you for the training process, provide you with test scenarios and sample exam questions, and lend you our top interview tips. Finally, we will break down the career options available for you as a social worker, give you a day to day analysis of what each role entails, and show you how you can rise within the field. By the end of this guide, you will have a comprehensive understanding of the social work sector, and hopefully gain an idea on whether this is the right career path for you.

As part of this product you
have also received FREE access
to online tests that will help you
to prepare for educational and
recruitment assessments.

To gain access, simply go to:

www.PsychometricTestsOnline.co.uk

Get more products for passing any
application, test or interview at:

www.how2become.com

CHAPTER 1

Am I right for the role?

As a social worker, the most important quality you
is a strong personality. The key is in the name, so
will be expected to socialise and interact with a variety of
ent people, many of them vulnerable and in need of mental and/
or physical assistance. It is extremely important that you remain
caring and non-judgemental in these types of situations. You may
not necessarily like the people you are working with; but remember
that you are there to do a job, and that job is to help them. In order to
do this, you must be a skilled communicator, who can readily adapt
to challenges and emotional situations. Furthermore, you need to be
strong-willed, and have the ability to make decisions which will not
always be popular. As a social worker, it is vital that every decision
you make is in the best interests of the people you are working with,
and will benefit them in the long term instead of simply pleasing
them in the short term. Finally, you need to be extremely organised.
Employees within the social sector are subject to huge amounts of
filing and paperwork. This paperwork can be used in a variety of
instances, such as court cases and child support reviews. Therefore
it is fundamental that you are organised, efficient and ready to take
on the challenge of preparing lengthy case supports and documents
for future inspection. You need to have great written communicational skills, as well as verbal.

In order to show you how these skills are relevant to the industry,
we have prepared some sample scenarios. These scenarios will
test your initial knowledge, and provide you with a beginner's insight into the type of decisions you will have to make whilst working
within the social sector. Read through each passage, and then do
your best to answer the related questions. Don't worry if you struggle with these, there is no right or wrong answer. The questions are
designed to give you an idea of how social work involves analysing
conflicting information. Highlight the most important information
in the passage, so that you can use it when it comes to answering
the questions.

SCENARIO 1:

Mr Smith has been admitted to hospital following a fall down the stairs. He is 76 years old, almost deaf, and lives on his own. His closest family live over 2 hours away, and up until now he has been coping independently, with a little help from his neighbours. The accident has effected Mr Smith's mobility, and he needs constant support to move around and perform basic activities such as going to the toilet. He is often confused, and in pain. The hospital medical team believe that Mr Smith should be placed into a care home. His family agree with this, as they do not feel they would be able to provide Mr Smith with adequate support if he returns home. Mr Smith has expressed clearly that he does not want to go into a home, and would rather his needs were met by a home care social worker. However, he is yet to be assessed by a social worker.

Using the above information, answer the following questions in the spaces provided.

What are the central issues/conflicts with the case?

Do you think Mr Smith has the capability to make the decision?
If so, why? If not, why not?

If you were assessing Mr Smith, what kind of things would you look for?

SAMPLE ANSWERS – SCENARIO 1:

What are the central issues/conflicts with the case?

The central issue in this case is the conflict of interest between Mr Smith, his family and the nursing staff. Mr Smith believes he is well enough to return home, and receive adequate home care support from local social workers. The medical staff, and Mr Smith's family, believe that he should be placed into a care home. The issue that must be determined is whether Mr Smith has the mental capacity to make this decision on his own. If it is determined that he does not have the capacity, then the decision will be taken out of his hands.

Do you think Mr Smith has the capability to make the decision?

There are two sides to this argument. Based purely on the above information, we are given little indication of Mr Smith's mental well-being, other than the sentence that reads, 'He is often confused'. Whilst he is clearly in great physical pain, and cannot hear, this does not mean that he is not mentally able to make decisions for himself. The fact that he has expressed himself clearly on the issue of his housing, indicates that he is indeed thinking logically in some respect. Therefore, based on the above passage, and no other given information, we should lean towards giving Mr Smith the benefit of the doubt. The assessment by the social worker will be the key to determining whether he is able to make the decision.

If you were assessing Mr Smith's situation, what would you look for?

As previously mentioned, the assessment will be fundamental in determining whether Mr Smith can make the decision himself. You would not only interview Mr Smith, but his family members and the medical team too. As a social worker, you should be paying partic-ular attention to the following aspects:

- Does Mr Smith have all of the information he needs to make the decision? For example, what are his expectations for when he returns home? Does he expect everything to return to the way it was before? What is his understanding of home care packages, and what is his understanding of living in a care home?

- Has his family been swayed by the advice of the medical team? What concerns do they have about his ability to live on his own, and why?

- Is Mr Smith thinking clearly and logically? Does he have a good and realistic understanding of the type of help he needs?

SCENARIO 2:

You are a social worker for a child named George. George is 14 years of age. One night, you get a phone call from the care home where George lives. He was seen drinking alcohol with a group of boys at the local park, and was brought back home by the police at 11pm. George is often missing from school, particularly during test days. He gets extremely agitated, and responds to teachers and care staff rudely. Both his school and care home have attempted varying degrees of reward and punishment, but nothing has worked. George is currently in his 6th home care placement.

Using the above information, answer the following questions in the spaces provided.

What are the central issues/conflicts with the case?

How would you approach George and engage with him?

What kind of programmes do you think could be set up to help George? Who would you contact in order to do this?

SAMPLE ANSWERS – SCENARIO 2:

What are the central issues/conflicts with the case?

The central issue in this case is that the individual in question is extremely uncooperative. Furthermore, he is a child, and therefore is largely unaware that his behaviour is both unacceptable, and damaging to himself. We need to find a way to show George the value of education, and the value of working with others. If George can identify how his behaviour is putting his future at risk, then he might be able to change his attitude.

How would you approach George and engage with him?

To answer this, use the information that we gave you earlier in the chapter. You can either take a 'firm but fair' approach to George, or a more relaxed, reassuring approach. Let's assume in this example, you visit the care home personally. Following this, you have a one-to-one sit down with George. Think about what kind of issues you need to raise, what needs to be identified and how you would persuade George to give your ideas a try. Remember that George may be unresponsive, or unwilling to cooperate. Therefore it is your job to get the information out of him.

It is important that you recognise:

- How George is feeling, and why.

- How he feels about his behaviour.

- Any future risks to George's wellbeing.

- George's attitude to you, and ways that your relationship can be improved.

- Any particular individuals who could act as a suitable role model for George.

- Why George is reluctant to attend school on testing days.

What kind of programmes do you think could be set up to help George? Who would you contact in order to do this?

One of the biggest problems is that George is failing to attend school. As a social worker, this should be a primary concern. A great way to improve this would be to liaise with the staff at the school to come up with a solution. We know that George gets nervous or agitated on testing days. Therefore, with the teaching staff, you should look into ways to make the testing process more comfortable for George. Perhaps he can take the test in a separate room, under more relaxed conditions. Perhaps he could be given more preparation time in the build up to tests, to make him feel better about taking them. Schools often have education-specific social workers or counsellors, posted within their premises. A good way to build up George's trust in the school might be to arrange weekly meetings between him and a selected member of the special services team.

Outside of education, you should ensure that George's care home is more pro-active in arranging activities and keeping him busy/giving him a social life. He is clearly mixing with the wrong type of people, and this will have negative long term effects. If possible, work to engage him with the other children at the care home; and if not, arrange for him to attend local youth groups and meetings within the community.

SCENARIO 3:

Susan is 13 years old, and has recently been placed with a new foster family. You are her new social worker, meeting her for the first time. Susan refuses to talk with her foster family. She had been living with her biological father, however he recently passed away. There were no other family members available to provide care for her. Since being fostered, Susan has had to move, start a new school, attend her father's funeral, and say goodbye to her friends.

Using the above information, answer the following questions in the spaces provided.

What are the central issues/conflicts with this case?

Is there any more information you would like to know about?

Since you are meeting Susan for the first time, what approach would you take with her?

<u>What would be your next steps in working with Susan?</u>

SAMPLE ANSWERS – SCENARIO 3:

What are the central issues/conflicts with this case?

The central issue in this case is that Susan has recently undergone many huge changes in her life in a short space of time. Since she is only 13 years old, this has been difficult for her to process. She is not speaking to her foster family and appears to have closed herself off.

Is there any more information you would like to know about?

It would be helpful, in this case, to get a little more background information on Susan. Prior to the first meeting, we should endeavour to discover why she was living with her father/where was her mother, how her father passed away (illness or sudden death), why no other family member was available to look after her, how far she has had to move away and how she is coping with her new school.

Since you are meeting Susan for the first time, what approach would you take with her?

As this is the first meeting, and we are dealing with a child who is in a particularly sensitive frame of mind, the best approach to take would be one that is soft and reassuring. In order to establish a future relationship with Susan, you need to introduce yourself as someone that she feels she can come to for advice and help. The more comfortable she feels in your presence, the more likely she is to open up to you. You should try to gain as much information as possible prior to the meeting, so that when it comes to asking questions, it does not feel as if you are interrogating her.

What would be your next steps for working with Susan?

After building a rapport with Susan, the next step would be to try and improve her relationship with her foster parents. You would do this, ideally, by meeting with each party separately and encouraging different methods of communication or engagement. Since at this point Susan is not even speaking with her foster parents, just getting her to talk to them would be a great starting point. It is also extremely important that you arrange some form of grief counselling for Susan. She is clearly not coping with her emotions particularly well, and therefore it is fundamental that she is given an outlet or someone she can talk to about her father's death. Failure to do this will only cause issues later along the line. Finally, it would be a good idea to either arrange a visit from her friends in her old neighbourhood, or try to arrange social activities between Susan and the children from her new community. In order to aid Susan's development, it is essential that she engages with other children and does not find herself in a position where she is lonely or friendless.

These three examples should give you an idea of the type of activities you will have to perform whilst working within the social sector. As you can see, there are no 'black and white' answers. Every scenario is unique and challenging; there will be both positive and negative reactions to every decision you make. If you struggled with the above three examples, don't worry. Our book will provide you with all of the information you need to confidently assess situations similar to those listed above, and make the right decisions. Critical thinking and situational judgement are both key components to this role. Throughout this book, you can expect to find multiple scenarios that are both similar and different in nature to those posted above. These will help you to test yourself as you progress through the guide, and become more proficient and capable at making judgements in each scenario.

In order to improve your understanding of situational judgements, we also offer online tests that will help you to improve your understanding within this area. You can practice an array of testing questions (not all specific to social work), in order to enhance your performance and understanding. For further details on these tests, please visit the following web address:

www.SituationalJudgmentTest.co.uk

CHAPTER 2

GCSE & A Level

Now that you have some idea of the personality requirements needed for the role, let's move onto the educational side of the process. In this chapter, we'll cover both GCSE and A Level Health and Social Care. We'll give you a detailed brief of each course, and any other options you might want to consider before you begin your degree, or move into the world of work. Finally, if you are someone who is in a different field altogether, and considering a change, we'll show you how to make this transition.

For most candidates, social work begins at GCSE. Health and Social Care has become a popular module on most college or school GCSE curriculums. Below we have laid out the format for a typical GCSE course, which takes two years to complete:

UNIT 1: HEALTH AND SOCIAL CARE: BEGINNING

This unit is usually assessed by a controlled examination, and will explore the following questions:

Who are the biggest users of care services, and why?

What type of care services are available?

What kind of values should care workers promote?

What skills and assets do care workers need to exercise whilst performing the role, and what are the best personal qualities to have?

UNIT 2: PERSONAL RELATIONSHIPS

This module is usually assessed by a 1 or 2 hour written examination, and will explore the following questions:

How can personal relationships affect an individual's mental growth and development; as well as their health and wellbeing?

How can life events and changes affect an individual's mental growth, health and wellbeing?

How can we offer support to individuals who are struggling with personal relationships, or changes in their life?

UNIT 3: HEALTH AND WELLBEING

This module is usually assessed by a controlled examination, and will explore the following questions:

How do we define the phrase 'physical health'?

What factors can positively and negatively impact an individual's physical health?

How do these factors damage an individual's physical health?

How can we support an individual by improving and maintaining their physical health?

UNIT 4: PROTECTING SERVICE USERS

This module is usually assessed by a written examination, and will explore the following questions:

Who requires protection, and how can we protect them?

How can first aid be used to deal with emergencies?

How can we identify potential threats to service users?

How can we act on these threats, to ensure users are safeguarded?

As you can see, initial Social Care modules also explore first aid and medical practice. Therefore taking this module at GCSE will not just prepare you for life as a social worker, but for other fields too. This can include working as a support assistant in a hospital, working in a nursery or even in medicine. The module will provide you with a solid platform on which you can build later success. Crucially, it also links in with many relevant A Levels. Subjects such as Psychology or Physiotherapy utilise the information picked up via this GCSE. Many GCSE modules also place their students on a short period of work experience, usually in a residential or nursing home. This is extremely useful for those who are looking to continue their career in the field. You are far more likely to be accepted onto a college or A Level course if you can demonstrate that you have some practical experience within the sector.

In the next section, we will give you a similar overview of an AS Level Social Work course, and following that, A Level Social Work course, so that you can see what the curriculum entails. You might experience any number of the modules we have listed, as well as any new modules that have recently been added onto the curriculum. When applicable, we have also included some practice questions, to give you some idea of how the modules will be assessed. The year in which you take your course will determine whether or not the listed module is compulsory, or optional.

HEALTH AND SOCIAL CARE: AS LEVEL

UNIT 1: CARE AND COMMUNICATION

This module provides an introduction for candidates to the key communication skills needed to work within the sector. The unit also introduces skills and techniques which can be used to provide care and support to individuals who require it. The assessment is coursework based, and will explore the following topics:

- The history of social work, government funding and statutory rights.

- The relationship between location and quality of life.

- The communicational skills needed to interact with and support service users, using workplace examples.

- The strengths and weaknesses of different caring and communication techniques, and an introduction to the evaluative skills needed to make key decisions.

UNIT 2: UNDERSTANDING HEALTH AND CARE

This module provides an introduction and understanding for students on an array of different health conditions, such as asthma, stroke, cancer and diabetes. The unit teaches candidates about the treatment and management of such conditions and the impact they can have on an individual's life. It also highlights the different healthcare experts with whom both patients and social workers might come into contact. This module is assessed by a written examination, and will explore the following topics:

- Various diseases and medical conditions; symptoms, identification and treatment.

- Managing these conditions within the context of everyday life.

- Various mental health issues and conditions; symptoms, identification and treatment.

- Managing these conditions within the context of everyday life.

PRACTICE QUESTIONS

The exam paper will usually start off each question with a case subject, the name of the condition they have, and the age of the individual in question. Using this information, you will be expected to produce appropriate, medically based responses.

QUESTION 1

Mary is 38 years old and has been diagnosed with breast cancer.

What is breast cancer?

Breast cancer is a malignant tumour that starts in the cells of the breast.

Identify two factors which might increase the risk of breast cancer.

You are at significant risk of breast cancer if you have a family history of the disease. Your risk of getting breast cancer can also increase with age.

Describe two symptoms of breast cancer.

The first symptom of breast cancer is a lump or area of thickened tissue on the breast. Other symptoms can include: a change of size in the breast, discharge or blood from the nipple, swelling or a lump in the armpit.

Give the name of two medical treatments Mary might have to deal with her cancer.

Two treatments that Mary might have to deal with her cancer are chemotherapy and radiotherapy.

QUESTION 2

Steven is 49 years old, and has been diagnosed with coronary heart disease. He never exercises, eats takeaway up to 4 times a week, and spends most of his time sitting on the sofa; smoking and watching television.

What is coronary heart disease?

Coronary heart disease is a disease where a substance called 'plaque' builds up inside the coronary arteries. This blocks the flow of blood to your heart muscles, and consequently stops your heart from receiving oxygen.

Identify three factors which might increase the risk of coronary heart disease.

Three factors which might increase the risk of coronary heart disease are smoking, high cholesterol and diabetes.

Describe <u>three</u> symptoms of coronary heart disease.

Symptoms of coronary heart disease can include: Tightness or pain in the chest, shortness of breath, or having a heart attack.

Give the name of <u>two</u> medical treatments Steven might have to manage his disease, and suggest <u>two</u> lifestyle changes he needs to make.

Coronary heart disease cannot be cured, but it can be managed. Steven can reduce his symptoms by exercising regularly, and stopping smoking. If his condition is particularly serious, he may need a heart transplant, or heart bypass surgery.

QUESTION 3

Bryan is 38 years old, and has been diagnosed with leukaemia.

What is leukaemia?

Leukaemia is a progressive disease in which bone marrow produces abnormal white blood cells, known as leukaemia cells.

Identify three factors which may increase the risk of leukaemia.

Three factors which may increase the risk of leukaemia are: A family history of the disease, exposure to certain chemicals or high levels of radiation, and smoking.

Describe four symptoms of leukaemia.

Four symptoms of leukaemia are: Frequent or unusual bleeding in areas such as the nose or gums, sweating, tiredness, and weight loss are also common symptoms.

Name the three treatment steps Bryan must take to combat his disease, and briefly explain the purpose of each step.

The three treatment steps are:

Induction Therapy - This kills leukaemia cells in the blood and bone marrow.

Consolidation Therapy - This kills any remaining cells that may fail to show up on scans.

Maintenance Therapy - This prevents any future cells from growing or forming again.

UNIT 3: LIFE CHALLENGES

This module provides an introduction for students to a range of different mental and physical conditions. More so than the previous module, this will focus on the way social workers and carers can aid individuals in dealing with their mental or physical defects. The unit teaches candidates about the treatment and management of such conditions and the psychological impact that they can have. This module is assessed by a written examination, and will explore the following topics:

- Various physical conditions, and the impact they can have on an individual's life.

- Managing physical conditions within the context of everyday life.

- Various mental health conditions, and the impact they can have on an individual's life.

- Managing mental health conditions within the context of everyday life.

PRACTICE QUESTIONS

Similarly to the previous written assessment, the exam will usually start off with a case subject. You will be told the physical or mental condition of the subject, and receive some situational background/history. You must then respond to the questions accordingly.

QUESTION 1
Sarah and Jason have a son, Paul. Paul has recently been diagnosed with cystic fibrosis.

What is cystic fibrosis, and how is it caused?

Cystic fibrosis is a genetic condition where the lungs and digestive system become filled with mucus. It is caused by a genetic mutation in the CFTR gene, which regulates the levels of sodium and chloride in cells.

How will cystic fibrosis affect Paul physically?

Cystic fibrosis will effect Paul in a number of ways. Firstly, he is likely to experience persistent coughing, as his body attempts to remove the mucus from his lungs. He is also likely to develop frequent lung and chest infections. Cystic fibrosis can also block the ducts to the pancreas. This may result in malnutrition, diabetes and an inability to gain weight. Furthermore, he is likely to be both infertile and incontinent, as a result of his illness.

How might the diagnosis affect Sarah and Jason?

Sarah and Jason are likely to receive the news with considerable shock. They may experience feelings of grief, loss, and even anger. In the long term, their social life is likely to suffer, as Paul will need constant support. This could also affect their careers, as at least one of them will have to be around to take Paul to physio and medical appointments. They may also be anxious and unsure as to what financial support they should get, and the cost of any necessary equipment. Finally, they would have to learn emergency procedures, such as percussion. This can be a physically demanding task. It involves rhythmically tapping or clapping on a sufferer's chest wall, in order to determine and clear the presence of excess fluid from their lungs.

What professionals might Sarah and Jason consult in regards to supporting their son? Name <u>three</u>.

Sarah and Jason might consult with: Their GP, a dietician or cystic fibrosis support groups/trusts.

QUESTION 2

Paula is 5 years old, and has Down's syndrome. She has recently started to attend primary school.

What is Down's syndrome, and what is it caused by?

Down's syndrome is a disorder that results in intellectual impairment and physical abnormalities. It is caused by an extra copy of chromosome 21 in a baby's cells.

How might Down's syndrome affect the rest of Paula's life?

If she has not already, Paula is likely to experience various health problems. She has an increased chance of developing lung and breathing infections, eye problems, ear problems and issues with her digestion. She may also be at risk of leukaemia, and could have learning difficulties.

Describe what policies a school can put in place to help Paula.

Paula's parents should work with the school to make sure that all her educational requirements are met. She may need to be put into a special class for children with learning difficulties. Using their pastoral and welfare system, the school should ensure that all staff are equipped with the knowledge and awareness of Paula's condition, and always have someone on hand to assist Paula if she is struggling. Furthermore, the school needs to be prepared to either send work home to Paula, or carry out independent catch up sessions for when she is missing from school. Finally, it would be useful if the school could invest in an experienced counsellor, who can provide emotional support to Paula whenever she needs it.

QUESTION 3

Richard has been diagnosed with Alzheimer's. He is 90 years old, and has no family. He is visited by his neighbour on a daily basis, and also receives home care. Recent investigations have suggested that Richard is no longer capable of living independently and should be placed into a care home. Richard does not want to move, and has refused to go.

What is Alzheimer's disease, and what are the key symptoms?

Alzheimer's disease is a form of dementia, whereby the brain cells of the sufferer slowly diminish. The key symptoms of Alzheimer's are: Memory problems; minor at first but increasing over time, confusion or hallucination, frequent personality changes, problems with speech and problems with moving around.

What factors increase the risk of getting Alzheimer's?

The risk of getting Alzheimer's increases with age. You are also more likely to suffer from the disease if you have a family history of the condition, if you have suffered significant head or brain injuries in the past, or if you have Down's syndrome.

How might having Alzheimer's disease make it difficult for Richard to live independently?

The disease will make it extremely difficult for Richard to make rational decisions. He will be constantly confused, disorientated and will be unable to deal adequately with his finances and bills. If he does injure himself, or contracts another illness, he will struggle to communicate this with those that could help him. He will be lonely, angry and depressed; especially since simple day-to-day activities will take him much longer to accomplish. He may also endanger himself, by forgetting to perform basic everyday safety checks on his home environment.

How might Richard's disease affect the emotional wellbeing of his neighbour?

Richard's neighbour will have to watch his friend further decline into dementia. This can be emotionally painful, and could have a profound effect. Due to the fact that Alzheimer patients are often prone to changes in personality, Richard's neighbour could find himself faced with shocking behaviour from his friend. He will no longer be able to socialise with Richard, and helping him will become more and more difficult.

How would the decision on whether Richard can live independently be made? In your answer you should refer to both the relevant legislation, and the professionals who will be involved in the decision making process.

Firstly, Richard would need to be diagnosed by his GP. Then, he would need to be assessed by social services on the safety implications of him remaining in his own home. Social services would also assess the location itself, in relation to the availability of nearby carers. If the decision is made to place Richard in a care home, then the Mental Health Capacity Act means that he will be directly involved in the decision making process. He will be placed in a home which meets the standards set by the Care Quality Commission (CQC), who inspect and regulate the quality of care homes.

UNIT 4: EDUCATING CHILDREN AND YOUNG PEOPLE

This unit introduces candidates to educational theory and practice. It requires candidates to plan and execute lessons. It also gives them crucial experience in interacting with and aiding younger people. The module is assessed via coursework, and will explore the following topics:

- The different methods used to teach children, including: Reflection and analysis, verbal instruction, experiential learning, research and reading.

- Lesson planning, styles of lesson and the pros and cons of each.

- Practical observation of lessons taught by qualified professionals in the field.

- Learning theory and practical application of these principles.

Provided you achieve respectable marks in your AS Level, you will then move on to A Level.

HEALTH AND SOCIAL CARE: A LEVEL

UNIT 1: LEARNING AND DEVELOPMENT

This unit provides a more advanced study into behavioural theory, learning and development. It will examine the impact of life events on an individual, lifestyle choices and physical or mental impairments. This module is assessed by a written examination, and will explore the following topics:

- Drug and substance abuse, anti-social behaviour and truancy.

- The impact of new-borns on a family, marriage, divorce and bereavement.

- The impact of being the victim/or witness to a crime, illness and accident, depression, mental health disorders or genetic predispositions.

PRACTICE QUESTIONS

The exam paper will usually start off each testing section with a case subject, the name of the condition they have and the age of the individual in question. Using this information, you will be expected to produce appropriate responses.

QUESTION 1

Samuel is 13 years old. He lives with his father, Gregg, and his father's new wife, Janine. Janine is expecting to give birth to twins in a few months' time. Samuel is very upset by this, he dislikes Janine and worries that the birth of the twins means he will get less attention. He has started truanting from school on a regular basis. When he attends school, he acts aggressively towards other students, and is rude towards his teachers.

The birth of a new sibling is a particularly significant life event. Name one other life event that may have resulted in/directly caused Samuel's bad behaviour.

Another event that may be responsible for Samuel's behaviour, is his father re-marrying.

Put yourself in Samuel's position. How do you think, that he thinks, the birth of his new siblings will affect him?

Samuel is worried that he will get less attention. Samuel might feel that he will be less loved than his new siblings, that he will be ignored and that Gregg and Janine will lose interest in him. Although he is probably too young to consider the financial implications of a new-born baby, he may be worried that less money will be spent on him as a result. This could affect him on occasions such as his birthday, or at Christmas.

Samuel is regularly truanting from school. How will this affect his future and how could it have damaging implications?

Samuel's lack of attendance at school will have a negative affect on his test and examination results, as he will spend less time learning. His school record would also be looked upon negatively by future employers. Detailed research has shown that there is a link between the amount of time a child spends out of school, and criminal or anti-social behaviour.

Samuel goes to see the school counsellor. What kind of approach could the counsellor use when dealing with Samuel? Explain the approach and what the benefits are of using this method?

The counsellor could use the behavioural approach. The behavioural approach explains abnormal behaviour via external events, and aims to improve or change this behaviour via conditioning/the carrot and stick approach. Tests and studies have shown that this is a fast working method for dealing with bad behaviour, as the focus is on adapting and changing particular behavioural traits, rather than treating the subject as if they personally are the issue. The biggest downside of this approach is that due to the focus on external events, sometimes problems that result from internal or biological factors may not be solved. This is a natural approach that works for people of all ages, and is very comfortable for younger or more anxious service users.

QUESTION 2

Wendy is 76 years old. Due to the fact she is struggling to cope whilst living on her own, her family have made the decision to place her in a residential care home. Wendy is very nervous about the move.

What impact could moving to a residential care home have on Wendy's mental and physical health?

Moving into residential care may affect Wendy in a number of ways. Physically, she will have to change both her sleeping and eating patterns, and will have more help with activities such as bathing and going to the toilet. Mentally, while she may see less of her family, and lose contact with some of her friends, she will meet new people, learn new skills and have less pressure put upon her.

Explain the humanist approach, and the ways in which care workers could use this to help Wendy come to terms with her situation.

The humanist approach believes that human behaviour is determined by our sense of self-concept. Individuals exist in a continually changing world of experience, that only we can understand. Therefore, if we feel unloved, or there is an incongruence between our self-concept and the way other people treat us, a state of anxiety or negative self-worth develops. This leads to cognitive dissonance. In order to lower anxiety, our self-concept must become more in line with our individual experiences. The humanist approach believes that by recognising your own flaws; you can become much more than you are, and change your life in the process.

In order to help Wendy deal with her anxiety towards the move, there are a number of things that the care workers can do:

- *They can take the time to talk to her and reassure her.*

- *They can take the time to aid her self-realisation, to make her understand her own flaws and the way she can help herself by accepting them.*

- *They can provide time and space for her to receive visits from friends and family.*

- *They can ensure there are always helpers available to assist her physically.*

Describe Eysenck's view on extroversion and introversion.

Eysenck linked extraversion and introversion with arousal. He described extraverts as showing low levels of cortical arousal, whereas introverts were over-aroused. As a result introverts will actively seek to lower their levels of arousal, whereas extroverts will seek to increase theirs through stimulating behaviour.

Describe Bandura's theory on the social learning perspective.

Bandura believes that behaviour is learned from the environment, through observational learning. His theory states that humans act as information thought processors, who actively consider the link between their behaviour and its consequences. In order to demonstrate this, he used children as an example. Firstly, he believes that children are more likely to imitate those who they consider similar to themselves; most often individuals of the same sex. They are more likely to continue this behaviour if the imitator themselves is rewarded, and if they personally are rewarded. For example, if a parent sees a girl hugging her friend and tells her 'that's very nice of you', the girl is more likely to continue her behaviour, since it has been reinforced. This also applies for punishment. However, Bandura believes that this reinforcement will have little to no impact if the reinforcement applied does not match with an individual's need; and is pointless if it does not lead to a positive change in the individual's behaviour.

UNIT 2: PRACTITIONER ROLES

This module provides candidates with an increased understanding of working with children, younger people and community justice. It will aim to give candidates a good idea of how well they would fit into a particular role, and in which area they would like to specialise. The assessment is coursework based, and will explore the following topics:

- *The history of social work.*

- *The way in which an individual's location can affect their quality of life.*

- *The way in which candidates can use their communicational skills to help service users.*

- *A variety of different social care techniques, and how we can use evaluative skills to come to unbiased decisions.*

UNIT 3: FOOD AND FITNESS

This module aims to provide candidates with a good understanding of dietary and nutritional requirements, in order to aid them in helping a range of different people. The unit will also study exercise routines, fitness and health. This module is assessed by a written examination, and will explore the following topics:

- Food components and how they affect health and well-being.

- Different types of physical exercise and how they affect the human body.

- Minerals and vitamins.

- The sociological and psychological benefits of exercise.

PRACTICE QUESTIONS

The exam paper will mix case subject tests, with factual information. Using the information provided by the exam, and learned on the course, you will be expected to produce appropriate responses.

QUESTION 1

What is aerobic fitness and how does it benefit the body? What type of activities are associated with aerobic fitness?

Aerobic fitness is exercise which increases the efficiency of your body in transporting oxygen and energy to vital areas such as the heart. It decreases the risk of stroke, hypertension and diabetes. Activities such as cycling, jogging, swimming and brisk walking can improve your aerobic fitness.

QUESTION 2

What are carbohydrates, and how can your body use them? In what food products would you find simple carbohydrates, and in what products would you find complex carbohydrates?

Carbohydrates are a large group of compounds which can be found in foods, living tissue, sugar, starch and cellulose. They are the biggest source of energy for the body, which turns them into glucose. This is then used to supply energy to your cells and organs. You would find simple carbohydrates in food such as fruit, vegetables and milk, and complex carbohydrates in whole grain bread, cereal and starchy vegetables.

QUESTION 3

Name three functions of calcium in the body. What would be the affect on an individual who has been deprived of calcium? List five good sources of calcium.

Calcium helps to:

-Build strong bones and teeth

-Regulate muscle contractions

-Ensure that blood flows and clots normally.

An individual who has been deprived of calcium might suffer from rickets or osteoporosis. Five good sources of calcium are: milk, cheese, soya beans, nuts and bread.

QUESTION 4

Explain how staying fit and healthy can positively affect an individual's emotional well-being?

Regular exercise gives people an improved sense of well-being. It allows for better sleep, a more relaxed and positive attitude towards their lives and eases stress and anxiety. As peoples physical attributes start to improve, they improve their self-esteem. Exercise can also work as a distraction from peoples worries or problems, and is sometimes used as a treatment for depression. It releases endorphins into your brain, which energise your body and make you feel good. Finally, studies have shown that staying fit and healthy increases your brain power, and sharpens your focus for intellectual tasks.

QUESTION 5

Miranda is a 45 year old woman. She weighs 17 stone and has been diagnosed with severe hypertension.

What is hypertension, and what types of exercise can be used to combat/regulate it?

Hypertension is the name for continuous high blood pressure. The best type of exercise to combat this is cardiovascular (aerobic) exercise. This will help to lower blood pressure and make Miranda's heart stronger. Miranda should be exercising for at least 30 minutes every single day, performing activities such as: jogging, walking, cycling, swimming and rowing.

UNIT 4: RESEARCH

This module aims to provide candidates with an understanding of research methods within the social sector. Using health, social care, community justice or young people, candidates will be required to undertake a period of independent research, and then carry out a study project to demonstrate their findings. The unit gives candidates the opportunity to explore future career pathways, and provides them with an initial idea of the area in which they would like to work. The module is assessed via a portfolio of evidence.

UNIT 5: MENTAL DISORDERS

This module aims to provide candidates with an understanding of a range of different mental health problems, causes and treatments. The unit will demonstrate the role of service professionals in dealing with these issues, and highlights the impact that mental health can have upon individuals, their friends and families. This module is assessed via a portfolio of evidence, and will explore the following areas:

- Various mental health issues and their symptoms.

- Causes of mental health issues and the impact they can have on an individual's behaviour.

- Treatment for mental health issues and the impact they can have on the carer themselves.

- Attitudes towards mental health and dealing with public ignorance.

UNIT 6: DIAGNOSIS AND TREATMENT

This module aims to provide candidates with an understanding of a range of different diagnostic techniques, common practice knowledge and principles. The unit will demonstrate how illness and other disorders can be dealt with and prevented, and highlight various treatment procedures. The module is assessed via a written examination.

PRACTICE QUESTIONS

The exam paper will usually start off each testing section with a case subject, the name of the condition they have and the age of the individual in question. Using this information, you will be expected to produce appropriate responses.

QUESTION 1

Susan is a 36 year old pregnant woman, attending her first ultrasound.

What is an ultrasound, and what kind of ultrasound will Susan have? Describe the procedure involved.

An ultrasound is a medical procedure which uses high frequency waves to produce live images from inside your body. It is the most common way to view a foetus prior to birth. Susan will have an external ultrasound.

To begin the ultrasound, Susan changes into a hospital gown. She then lies down on a table whilst a sonographer applies a lubricating jelly to her skin. This helps with the sound waves, and reduces friction between the ultrasound transducer and her skin. Once the transducer has been placed onto her belly, it sends high frequency sound waves though her body. When the waves hit an object such as an organ or bone, they echo. The echo is reflected back into the computer, and produces images. The doctor cleans off the gel from Susan's stomach, allows her to leave and then checks the images. He comes back half an hour later with the images.

Name two other types of ultrasound. Describe what they are used for, and the procedure involved in each.

The two other types of ultrasound are an internal ultrasound, and an endoscopic ultrasound.

An internal ultrasound allows a doctor to look at an individual's organs in more detail; such as the prostate or womb. The patient will lie on their back or side with their knees drawn to their chest. The doctor will then place a probe in the vagina or rectum, and feedback images to a medical screen.

An endoscopic ultrasound is another method for studying a patient's organs, however this examination studies areas such as the stomach or throat. You will normally swallow the endoscopic probe, which the doctor then pushes down towards your stomach. The endoscope will send ultrasound waves around the body, and feedback images onto the screen.

Name <u>one</u> risk typically associated with these two types of scan.

One minor risk that can often result from an internal or endoscopic exam, is internal bleeding.

QUESTION 2

Perry is a 38 year old man, who has gone to see his GP to have his blood pressure tested.

Describe the way in which Perry's GP would measure his blood pressure.

There are two ways in which Perry's GP might measure his blood pressure. Firstly, there is the manual method. This involves the following:

First, an inflatable cuff is wrapped around Perry's upper arm and held in place with Velcro. There are two tubes leading out from the cuff, one which leads to a rubber bulb; and the other which leads to a container of mercury at the bottom of a glass column. The pressure contained within the cuff is displayed via the mercury metre. Air is then blown into the cuff, increasing the pressure and tightening the cuff around the arm. Perry's doctor uses a stethoscope to listen to the pulse of his arm, whilst the air is being released. He will measure both the systolic, and diastolic pressure. The alternative method to this is to use an electronic blood measuring device, where Perry simply puts his arm into a machine, which squeezes and then reads the pressure automatically.

How often is it recommended that Perry comes in to check his blood pressure? What medical issues might have prompted Perry to come in?

If he does not have high blood pressure, then it is recommended that Perry gets tested once every five years. However, this can be reduced as he gets older, and may be shortened up to once every single year. Symptoms such as: a persistent headache, blurred vision, nosebleeds and shortness of breath are all indications of high blood pressure, and may have persuaded Perry to visit his doctor.

WORK EXPERIENCE

During your AS and A Level modules, it is a fantastic idea to try and gain as much practical experience as you possibly can. The majority of university courses look for a period of 3 months or 60 days minimum field experience from their applicants. Therefore if you are looking to take social work to a higher level, then any voluntary or paid work will be extremely useful when it comes to applying for university. This shows a sustained commitment to the cause, and that you are not someone who will shy away from hard work. The process of finding social or pastoral experience should be fairly simple. There are plenty of options available for aspiring candidates, these include:

- Residential or day care work.

- Teaching.

- National and local organisations, such as CSV
  http://www.csv.org.uk

You can also use newspaper articles, magazines and other local media to find vacancies in your area. Organisations are always looking for enthusiastic volunteers to join their team. This will give you vital practical experience in what is an emotionally difficult role, and better prepare you for some of the challenges ahead. Universities are looking for candidates who can demonstrate their passion for the role, through both educational and personal experience. For certain universities, you might even be expected to attend an interview prior to being accepted. Later in this guide, we will devote an entire chapter to social work interview questions, answers and preparation techniques. This will aid you in both the early and later stages of your career.

OTHER OPTIONS

Following on from your A Levels, you might also be interested in taking an apprenticeship. An apprenticeship in social work will provide you with the work experience and qualifications needed to gain employment in the sector, whilst earning a wage. Most apprenticeships last for 2 years, and are a great introductory pathway for beginners.

In chapter 9 of this guide, we've provided with you three detailed 'day in the life' segments, which will highlight some of the work you'll be expected to do whilst employed within the social sector. If you are interested in taking an apprenticeship, this will be really useful for you, as it will demonstrate some of the work you'll be assisting with as an apprentice. Applying for a social work apprenticeship is extremely simple, usually your local authority will advertise jobs on their website, or you can perform a quick internet search to bring up hundreds of different options. As an apprentice, you'll likely be performing a whole range of tasks, so therefore it's a great way to challenge yourself and help you determine your future career path.

In order to get a job as a social worker, you must be in possession of the relevant qualifications, which can only be obtained by reaching the highest level of college, taking a university degree or an apprenticeship.

CHAPTER 3

College

College courses in social work provide candidates with the same opportunity that they would get at A Level, and offer the opportunity to move up and take higher qualifications such as Level 3. The first step when applying for colleges is to fill in an online application form. This can be done via the college website. Once your application has been filled in, it will be looked over by the college admissions team, and then passed over to the relevant department. To help you decide which college you should apply for, it is advised that you either go into the college, or visit their website. There you will be able to find and download a full prospectus for the year ahead. The majority of colleges will look for GCSE grades in Maths, English and Social Care, and may also require some relevant work experience within the social sector.

The Application

Generally, if you are applying for a college, you should expect a similar form to this:

Full name:

Title: Mr/Mrs/etc

DOB:

Address:

Postcode:

Gender:

Ethnicity:

Prior Attainment Level:

Are you a British Citizen:

Have you been a resident of the UK/EU for 3 years:

Are you, or have you ever been in local authority care:

Do you have any unspent criminal convictions?

You will then be given a question in regards to your interest in the subject, and enthusiasm for the course. This is the most important part of the application, and here at How2Become, we have prepared a sample answer that you can use as a basis for your own.

The question might look something like this:

'Tell us why you should be given a place on the course you have chosen, and why we should consider you for the course. You should outline your career ambitions, personal interests and any work experience, including voluntary work.'

A question such as this is looking for a number of different things from the applicant. The key word here is 'you'. The course administrators are clearly looking for a quality that sets you apart from other applicants. While they will obviously be accepting a number of different applicants, the emphasis in answering this question should be upon your own strengths, and how they can be applied to this course. You, the reader of this book, already have a distinct advantage in that we have prepared you with the knowledge of what qualities a social worker requires. You should be:

- Willing to take on difficult challenges.

- Highly relatable and empathetic.

- Sociable, caring and comfortable with people.

- Organised, and capable of making tough decisions.

This question requires an answer in regards to your career ambitions, personal interests and work experience. It is a good idea in this case to set your ambitions high. By telling the course providers that it is your future aim to work full time within the social sector, or specialise at a higher level, you are letting them know that you are an applicant with a strong, passionate and enthusiastic attitude towards the course. You need to demonstrate hard work in order to achieve great results. A lack of answer to this question will serve as an immediate red flag to the department. They are looking for interested and ambitious candidates who will go on to represent the college at a later level. You should therefore tailor your answer towards higher ambitions within the field. If you have relevant educational experience, particularly English and Maths, it would also be extremely useful to mention this.

In terms of both personal interests, and work experience, you should also take the same positive approach. If you are someone with a lack of direct work experience, then it is okay to use indirect, or unpaid experience. For example, you may have spent time counselling your friends or family, or looking after an elderly relative. If you can give examples of where you have demonstrated behaviour that is befitting of the course values, you will massively increase your chances. Customer service related experience will also help you in this case, since you need to be able to show that you have a previous history of working with and helping people.

Using all of the above information, write out your answer to the question below, and then see how it compares with the sample response on the next page:

Tell us why you should be given a place on the course you have chosen, and why we should consider you for the course. You should outline your career ambitions, personal interests and any work experience, including voluntary work.

Sample Response

Dear Sir/Madam,

I am writing to apply for a place on your course in 'Health and Social Care'. I feel that I would make a fantastic candidate, and already possess many of the qualities needed to succeed within this field. I am shortly due to receive my results for GCSE's in Maths, English and Social Care, and I believe that these studies will really help me when it comes to taking your course. I'm a caring, empathetic person who loves new challenges and helping people. One day I would love to specialise in childcare, and I have lots of past experience babysitting for my neighbours and family. Furthermore, during my GCSEs, I have spent some time performing work experience in a care home, and therefore I have a knowledge of caring for a wide range of individuals. I'm now looking to pick up the valuable tools and further my experience needed to work within the social sector. I believe that your college is the best place for me to learn, and I would be very grateful if you could consider my application.

Yours sincerely,

As you can see, we have put ourselves across as someone who would be perfect for the industry, and more importantly, someone who is extremely interested in the course. In some college application forms, you may be asked 3 or 4 questions. Below we have listed some of the further questions you might expect to see, and included sample responses to each of them. As before, our responses are generalised to all types of college courses and applications.

Describe a situation where you have worked with people who are different from you in relation to age, background or gender.

This question has been designed to assess your ability to work with others, regardless of their background, age or gender. Many organisations will want to see evidence of where you have already worked with people of different ages, sexes, sexual orientation, backgrounds, cultures and religious beliefs. Remember to be specific in your responses, and relate them to a particular situation. An example of a bad response would be – 'I am comfortable working with people from different backgrounds and have done this on many occasions'. This type of response is not specific and does not relate to a particular situation. You need to back up your reasoning with clear examples.

Sample Response

'Whilst working in my current role as a sales assistant I was tasked with working with a new member of the team. The individual in question had just started working with us and was unfamiliar with the role. She was from a different background and appeared to be very nervous. I tried to comfort her and told her that I was there to support her through her first few working days and would help her get her feet under the table. I fully understood how she must have felt. It was important that I supported her and helped her through her first few days at work. As a result of my actions the lady settled into work well and is now very happy in her role. We have been working together for 3 months and have built up a close professional and personal relationship.'

Describe a situation where you have worked closely with other people as part of a team.

The ability to build working relationships with your colleagues is very important. Never underestimate how important teamwork is within an organisation. Try to think of a situation when you have worked as part of a team, maybe to achieve a common goal or task. Remember to be specific about a particular situation and avoid the pitfall of being too generic.

Sample Response

'I recently volunteered to work with a new member of our team at work. The task required us to successfully complete a stock-take of the entire warehouse within a short timeframe. The reason why I volunteered for the task is because I am a conscientious person who enjoys working with other people, and carrying out tasks to a high standard. Initially I showed the new team member how to stock-take in a professional manner in accordance with company guidelines. He had never carried out this type of work before and I wanted to ensure he was comfortable with the task, and that he was doing it correctly. Once I had achieved this we both then set about methodically working through each aisle, stocktaking as we went along. Periodically we would stop to ensure that the task was being done correctly. At the end of the specified timeframe we had completed the stock-take and were able to provide accurate figures to our line manager. Whilst working as a team member, I always concentrate on effective communication, focusing on the task at hand and providing support to team members who require assistance.'

Describe a situation where you have had to remain calm and controlled in a stressful situation.

This does not necessarily have to be in a work situation, but it may be during leisure time or at home. Be careful not to answer this question generically. Focus on a particular situation that you have encountered recently.

Sample Response

'Whilst driving home from work, I came across a road accident. I parked safely and went over to see if I could help. An elderly lady was in one of the cars suffering from shock. I remained calm and dialled 999 asking for the Police and Ambulance services. Once I had done this I then gave basic First Aid to the lady and ensured that the scene was safe. The reason I took this course of action was because when I arrived people were starting to panic, so I knew that somebody needed to take control of the situation. By remaining calm and confident I was able to get help for the lady. As a result of my actions, the emergency services soon arrived and the lady was taken to hospital. The police then took some details of my actions and thanked me for my calm approach and for making the scene safe.'

COLLEGE INTERVIEW

If your application is successful, you will then be invited to attend an interview with one of the senior teaching staff at the college.

The first thing you will be required to do upon arrival at many of these interviews, is to fill in a questionnaire. Similarly to the original application, this will test your prior knowledge of the social sector, and your enthusiasm for the course. We have tracked down a sample questionnaire, and provided sample responses to each question, to aid you in your preparation for this process.

SAMPLE QUESTIONNAIRE

Please answer the following questions as clearly as possible:

1. Do you have any medical issues, or medical history that we should know about?

Always ensure you are honest with the institution, as this question is asked for your welfare/benefit.

2. What hobbies/interests do you have?

Similarly to the way we answered in the initial application form, here you should tailor your answer to the question. Show an interest in the subject, but keep your answer short and succinct.

'I am very interested in social care and helping others. I regularly babysit for friends and family and absolutely love children. That is one of the biggest reasons I am considering childcare as a potential career.'

3. Why have you chosen social work as a career?

This is a great chance for you to tell the institution about your plans and future ambitions, and let them know how much you care about the subject. Once again, keep your answer short, succinct and on topic.

'I have always been a social and relatable person, and a job which allows me to help and meet with new people is very appealing. I have considerable amounts of experience in helping both children and the elderly, and would love to further these skills. I believe that I could learn so much from this course, and ultimately want to take the knowledge I pick up from your college and apply it into the social workplace.'

4. **What is the most important skill needed to work within the social sector?**

- Communication skills.

- Acting skills.

- Foreign language skills.

- Entertainment skills.

Answer: Communication Skills

5. **Why is it essential that you are an empathetic and relatable person?**

- To ensure that you treat all service users fairly.

- To ensure service users like you.

- To find out what service users did at the weekend.

Answer: To ensure that you treat all service users fairly.

6. **Why is good communication essential for social workers? Give one workplace example of how good communication is important.**

'It is important that social workers communicate effectively with service users, to ensure that they have all of the information available to make an informed decision. A good example would be when deciding whether elderly individuals should be placed into care. The social worker would have to communicate effectively with the individual in question, to decide whether they have the mental capacity to make the decision for themselves. The social worker would also have to communicate with the individual's family and doctors, to gain as much information as possible prior to making a decision.'

7. Give two examples of good behaviour, and two examples of bad behaviour, when working within the social sector.

<u>Good:</u>

<u>Bad:</u>

This is a harder question, which requires prior knowledge of the industry. Below we have listed a number of different answers to this question, for both good and bad.

SAMPLE ANSWERS:

Good	Bad
• Being patient and understanding with all types of people.	• Being rude to service users, judging them on a personal level.
• Making sure that you have all of the facts from all involved parties, prior to making decisions.	• Failing to communicate effectively with all involved parties prior to making decisions.
• Making unbiased, fair decisions that are in the best interests of the related individual.	• Making decisions that are based on either your like or dislike for the individual, or decisions which are predicated on inaccurate information.

Good	Bad
• Ensuring that the individual in question has knowledge of all of the facts and understands why you have made your decision, prior to any changes being made. • Ensuring that you have logged and filed all of the case information for future review or use. • Ensuring that you check up on the client, following any changes.	• Failure to inform the service user of the decision you have made and the reasons why you have made it. • Failure to log and file case material for future use or review. • Failure to arrange follow up appointments with service users after any applied changes.

Upon completion of this test, you will then be required to pass a verbal interview with one of the lecturers. This is great practice for both work based interviews, and university applications. Most universities will require you to take an interview prior to starting an undergraduate degree in social work, in order to assess your prior knowledge. Therefore, you can use these initial college questions as a starting point for the questions you should expect to see later on. If you perfect your answers here, you will have a much easier time gaining work in the industry when your course has finished. We have included direct interview tips at the end of this chapter, and during the next few chapters of this guide.

COLLEGE INTERVIEW QUESTIONS

After completing your questionnaire, you will be invited into a room which will contain either 1 or 2 lecturers. They will shake your hand, offer you a seat and then begin their questioning. There are a great number of things they could ask, so it is best to be prepared for all types of questions. With this in mind, use the following general interview based questions to get yourself ready for the process:

1. Do you know what the course entails?

If you are someone who has done their research prior to the interview, then you should have no problem with this question. By showing the interviewer that you have researched the course and understand what it will involve, you are showing them that you are an interested and enthusiastic student.

'Yes, I picked up a prospectus prior to this interview. I know that this course involves communication skills, health, safety and security procedures, anatomical development, physiological development and human rights. I'm considering specialising in childcare later in my career, so I'm hoping it will aid me in this endeavour.'

2. Why do you want to take the course?

The interviewer here is looking for a clear and concise idea of what aspects of social work the candidate is particularly interested in, and a rough outline of their future ambitions. There is nothing worse than saying 'I don't know' in an interview, as this tells the interviewer that you are not interested in the course, and don't care much about the subject. Don't be scared to sound ambitious, the college want people who are eager and willing to learn.

'I would love a place on this course because I think it is the best way to prepare me for a future as a social worker. I'm really interested to learn more about human rights and communicational techniques,

and hope to apply these someday when working in the field. I'm hoping to pass Level 2, and then move onto Level 3. Following that, I'd like to take a degree in social work at university.'

3. What makes you a good candidate for this course?

This is a question you should expect to hear in every interview. It is a great question for you, because it allows you to sell yourself to the interviewer. By now, you should have a pretty good idea of what qualities a social worker needs. You should tailor these qualities into your answer, and make yourself sound like the perfect student. While you should try to come across as confident and enthusiastic, don't be afraid to flatter the institution a little either.

'I am not just a great candidate for this course, but as a social worker in general. I am a really caring, empathetic and relatable individual who loves meeting and helping people. My time spent babysitting, and in an elderly care home, has shown me that this is the field I would love to work in full time. I've still got a great deal to learn, and this course will benefit me in that respect. I really believe that this is the best place for me to utilise my skills and enhance my knowledge.'

4. Tell me about yourself.

This is similar to the last question, but often this particular question is an attempt by the interviewer to get to know whether your personality is the right fit for the industry. Particularly in social work, you need to have a strong personality to cope with the emotional demands of the role.

'I'm a very caring, hard-working and professional person, and I love helping people. I've been brought up under the rule that you should treat others as you would like to be treated, and I try to apply this to every situation that I encounter. Working as a babysitter has provided me with great experience in a field that I would be really interested in pursuing, and I hope to further my understanding of social work to one day become successful and qualified within the field.'

Before your interview, practice using the mirror at home. Make sure that you are able to put your answers across clearly and slowly. Due to nerves, many people talk too fast in interview situations. Remember that the most important thing in this interview is that the interviewer sees you as a friendly, caring and interested candidate. They are not there to judge, dismiss or undermine you, they are primarily there to see whether you are a suitable candidate for the role.

In the next section, we'll give you a detailed overview of the type of work you should expect to find on a college course in social work.

HEALTH AND SOCIAL CARE

The majority of college courses have three or four stages that candidates can complete. The number you must complete depends upon your GCSE grades and previous experience.

Entry Level 1: This is an entry level course for candidates with lower GCSE grades, and will give candidates basic skills in the childcare, health and social sectors. The central aim of this course is to provide candidates with the skills needed to progress to Level 2. Candidates at this level are also required to take English and Maths at the college in question, to enhance their employability. Most colleges will look for applicants who have GCSE grades from G-E and above.

Level 2: This is the most common entry point for candidates, and provides them with more advanced skills than in Level 1. The course will highlight a wide variety of topics and areas within the social care sector; and will utilise more practical skills and work experience than in Level 1. Candidates who are successful at this level will have the chance to move up to Level 3. Depending on your GCSE grade, you may also be expected to take an English and Maths course alongside this, in order to enhance your employability. Most colleges will look for applicants who have GCSE grades from D-C and above, or have taken the aforementioned Level 1 Diploma.

Level 3: This is a more advanced course, and provides candidates with an in-depth understanding of all roles within the social sector. The course is often done over 2 years, with candidates first taking an initial diploma which will provide them with a set amount of credits, and then extending their diploma in the second year. After you have completed this course, you will have the opportunity to move up to take a HND (Higher National Diploma) in health and social care. Most colleges will look for applicants who have GCSE grades from grade C and above; or have taken the aforementioned Level 2 Diploma.

HND: A Higher National Diploma (HND) in health and social care provides candidates with a comprehensive and complete understanding of the social sector, as well as the qualifications needed to apply for roles within the industry. The course will teach candidates management and supervisory skills which will prepare and help them to gain junior level social care jobs. This course also furthers a candidate's chances of being accepted onto a related university programme. Most colleges will look for applicants who already have diplomas in relevant subjects, and an extended level 3 diploma as previously mentioned.

MODULES

The following is a generalised list of modules which you might expect to encounter on a college course in health and social care. All colleges will have varying prospectuses and modules for each level, so therefore it is highly advised that you check with the college itself before applying. The aim of this list is to give you a broad overview of how college modules are assessed and what type of work you will be expected to undertake.

COMMUNICATION SKILLS:

This is one of the core modules that all colleges will run on their programme. It will help candidates to understand how different forms of communication can be used within the health and social sectors, how they can improve their own communicational ability, and the importance of communication in order to provide service users with the best possible help. The unit will look at communicational barriers, the effects that that both good and bad communication can have on service users and how communication works within a legal setting. Finally, the unit will examine how technology can be used to communicate with service users. This unit is normally assessed by coursework, written reports and portfolios.

Below we have provided you with some examples of how you might be assessed. You might experience any combination of these assessments, or even completely different assessments, on your college module.

Guidebook: One of the things that you might be asked to do for the assessment is to produce a scenario based guidebook, which explains communication and caring strategies to a new member of staff. You should pay particular attention to presentation, ensuring that the guidebook is written in a simple and clear format.

Written Report: Another thing you might be asked to do is to write a report on how you have personally used communication skills whilst caring for or helping others. This does not necessarily have to be a factual account, just as long as you can show that you have a good knowledge of the skills required. You will be expected to make reference to various theories: such as the humanist and behaviourist approach, communication techniques, advantages and disadvantages of these techniques, and demonstrations on how you have overcome issues in regards to communication and confidentiality.

Presentation: You might also have to produce a presentation that evaluates how communication can be used to deal with issues in areas such as race, gender, religion and disability. You will be asked to choose a particular topic on which to focus your investigation, and then collect detailed research notes on your chosen topic.

Essay: Essays are a common form of assessment. One topic on which you might be asked to write an essay in this particular module, is communication vs legislation. This will ask you to write an essay based on your experience, and how legislation can sometimes hinder the communication process within the social sector. It will require you to demonstrate examples of when you personally have had to deal with difficult legislation or workplace rules, but have still managed to provide an optimum service that kept within the legal boundaries.

Technological Report: Since this module will examine the way in which technology can be used to communicate within the social sector, you are likely to encounter an assessment based on this. Usually, this will take the form of a written report which shows how common software and programmes, such as Microsoft Word, can be used within health and social care. You will be required to demonstrate your capability in using all elements of software, such as Word, PowerPoint and Excel. Therefore, in your report, you should make use of every single one of the core programmes to produce a related part of the project. For example, you might create a presentation on your report using PowerPoint, an Excel spreadsheet to display the data you have collected, and a written summary using Word.

HEALTH AND SAFETY:

This is another core module that you should expect to find on all college courses in health and social care. It aims to help candidates understand health and safety in the workplace, and teaches them responsibility and risk assessment skills. The knowledge gained in this module will not just be essential for working within the social sector, but in any future job role. Candidates will develop their knowledge of health and safety legislation within the social setting, understand how this legislation affects their role as a social worker and how they can implement this legislation when working. Finally, candidates will learn the importance of organisation, keeping service user records and monitoring services. This unit is normally assessed by coursework, written reports and portfolios.

Below we have provided you with some examples of how you might be assessed during this module. You might experience any combination of these assessments, or even completely different assessments, on your college module.

Written Report: One of the most common ways that your course will assess this module, is through a written report which demonstrates a detailed understanding of health and safety in the workplace. Since health and social care is both a practical, and learning based course, the modules will often ask you to draw on your real life work experience as a basis for your essays. In your report, you might be asked to describe the legislations that are relevant to your current workplace, talk about the policies and procedures which are used, and how responsibilities are divided amongst the team within the workplace. You will be required to demonstrate good knowledge of where health and safety is most relevant within your workplace, and the particular priorities of the institution for which you work.

Risk Assessment: Since this module requires a knowledge of practical applications, you are likely to be tested on your ability to assess and care for service users. One of the most common assessment procedures is via a practical risk assessment on an individual within your workplace. This might take the form of a care plan, or report, which describes how you will implement your organisations health and safety policies in a certain situation which requires care and assistance. The report might discuss any conflicts or moral dilemmas with the case at hand, and how you have made key decisions in order to rectify these situations. You might also be asked to produce a report that concentrates on one particular health and safety policy that is present within your work place, how it impacts the service users and social workers within that sector, and why it is important.

Essay: You are also likely to write at least one essay for this module. There are any number of potential topics which may come up, but in general you should expect that all of your essays will either focus upon one particular aspect of health and safety, or ask you to give a broader overview of all aspects of health and safety. This can include: individual responsibility, organisation, risk assessment, review practice and personal reflection.

PUBLIC HEALTH:

This module links in with the previous, and aims to help candidates understand public health and the methods that can be used to prevent illness and disease from spreading in communities. Candidates will investigate and research the different ways in which different agencies combat disease and illness, the different types of illnesses; both infectious and non-infectious, regional and international perspectives on health, social care and disease, and how these can affect the wellbeing of service users in social care settings. This unit is normally assessed by coursework, written reports and portfolios.

Below we have provided you with some examples of how you might be assessed. You might experience any combination of these assessments, or even completely different assessments, on your college module.

Report: During this module you are likely to be asked to demonstrate your knowledge of current approaches towards disease. This usually takes the form of a written report, which focuses on specific diseases and the global and regional prevention policies in place to combat these diseases. Candidates will need to display a good understanding of organisations such as the World Health Organisation, voluntary trusts, the European Union and other international support groups. When focusing on non-contagious diseases, you will be expected to include research on health problems such as obesity; and how you can help service users to overcome these issues.

Presentation: Another popular assessment method on this module, is via scenario-based presentations. These will put you in the position of a health and safety official within your community, and may require you to do any number of things; from presenting and requesting help from your local authority, to containing the spread of particular medical problems within the area. To accompany this presentation, you will normally have to produce an additional written report summarising your key points and content.

Poster: In order to further your presentational skills, you may also be asked to produce a poster. Usually this will be related to something within your own work experience, so for example you might be asked to produce a poster on how individuals within your own care sector can be protected or safeguarded.

HUMAN RESOURCES:

This unit aims to provide candidates with an understanding of the human resource system within the social sector. It will highlight areas such as recruitment and management of workers within the social care workplace, and examine different ways of supporting employees. The module will demonstrate the value of teamwork and how different members of the social sector can work together to contribute the best possible service to individuals. Finally, the module will examine organisational techniques and show how these can be used and are relevant to legal proceedings. This unit is normally assessed by coursework, written reports and portfolios.

Below we have provided you with some examples of how you might be assessed. You might experience any combination of these assessments, or even completely different assessments, on your college module.

Presentation: For this module, you will normally be placed in a role and then asked to deliver a presentation based on the requirements of the role. For example, you might be asked to review a particular aspect of management, such as recruiting staff members. In your presentation you will have to demonstrate that you have a good understanding of all of the factors needed to make an unbiased and fair review. You will also have to draw up a table that demonstrates the factors you have taken into consideration and show how you have used legislation to come to a final decision.

Report: In this unit, you will normally need to produce a piece of work that explains how management and teamwork can affect professionals within health and social care. You will need to demonstrate a good understanding of behavioural theory, team building methods and management techniques. In your report, you will need to identify theories of leadership, the positives and negatives of each theory, and show how you have applied at least one of these theories in a workplace setting.

Essay: You may also be asked to write an essay. There are a wide range of potential topics, but is it likely that the essay title will focus specifically on topics relating to management and staff care. You will need to demonstrate good understanding of how management within the health and social care sector can deal effectively with their staff. Furthermore, you will need to show how senior management can help with training and individual needs, and identify different strategies for promoting positive developments within the health and social care workplace.

HEALTH AND SOCIAL CARE: MODERNITY

This unit aims to provide candidates with an understanding of modern issues within health and social care. It will explore areas such as public perception, how health and social care is presented within the media, and how social workers can disprove negative stereotypes associated with the role. This unit is normally assessed by coursework, written reports and portfolios.

Below we have provided you with some examples of how you might be assessed. You might experience any combination of these assessments, or even completely different assessments, on your college module.

Report: Usually you will be asked to prepare a portfolio and report on the public perception of a specific area of interest. You can use newspapers, the internet, books and other sources to accumulate a portfolio of evidence which supports your argument. Your portfolio will be handed in alongside a written report which explains the evidence that you have accumulated.

Essay: This will normally explore the broader spectrum of the module. For example, you might be asked to write an essay on how the media portrays certain issues in health and social care, and explain how this can affect public perception. To pass this essay, you will to demonstrate that you have a good understanding of a wide variety of issues and a good knowledge of relevant case history to back up your ideas.

Presentation: Following these two exercises, you will be asked to perform a presentation on your research findings. You will be required to show that you have thought about possible improvements and recommendations for positive change in your chosen area, and the consequences of your conclusions.

RESEARCH:

This unit aims to provide candidates with an understanding of the research and decision making skills needed to work within the social sector. It will show candidates how to make important enquiries, analyse service user related responses and undertake critical research. Finally, it will explore the legalities and ethical aspects of research, and examine data collection techniques. This unit is normally assessed by coursework, written reports and portfolios.

Below we have provided you with some examples of how you might be assessed. You might experience any combination of these assessments, or even completely different assessments, on your college module.

Report and Proposal: In this task, you will be asked to research and prepare a particular project for approval or hypothetical funding. You need to construct a lengthy report, supported by your research; which highlights the reasons why your project is important and how it can be carried out. You will need to take into account issues relating to the ethics of the project, legal restrictions and identify a clear reason for why you have chosen your project.

Essay: For the essay portion of this module, you will need to produce a piece of work which relates to your research and data. You will need to prepare and collect a sample of data prior to the essay, and then elaborate on the results and your methods in the assessment. You should demonstrate a good knowledge of the advantages and disadvantages of the methods that you have used to collect your data, and display an understanding of how your research methods could be improved, if you were to do it again.

Presentation: Following the previous two tasks, you will be required to present your findings to a larger group. You will be expected to have a good knowledge of the methods used, and the conclusions that you reached in each of the previous assessments.

LEARNING THEORY:

This unit will provide candidates with an understanding of how health and social workers can aid service users in the learning environment. This will also demonstrate communication and learning methods which can be applied in the workplace environment; to help other health and social workers. This module is usually optional, and mostly benefits candidates who are interested in becoming learning support assistants, or working within the educational system. The unit is normally assessed by coursework, written reports and portfolios.

Below we have provided you with some examples of how you might be assessed. You might experience any combination of these assessments, or even completely different assessments, on your college module.

Report: In this task, you will usually be asked to report on different theories of learning and explain how they can be applied within the context of your own workplace. You should reference examples of how you have used the theories taught by the module to aid service users.

Guidebook: One of the most popular assessment methods on this module is via a guidebook, pamphlet or brochure. These will relate specifically to learning theory, and cover various scenarios that can take place within the workplace. Your book should illustrate how each learning theory can be applied, advice for applying the theory and how to identify which theory to use. The type of pamphlet produced will depend specifically on your course provider. For example, you might be asked to produce a booklet which explains learning theory to newer members of staff, or you might be asked to produce a booklet which is aimed at service users themselves.

Training: This is a practical assessment which will examine your ability to train and support others in the workplace. You will be asked to produce and then demonstrate a training plan for a specific task in the health and social care sector; for example helping a client go to the loo, dealing with relatives or interviewing a service user. Your plan should demonstrate that you have a broad understanding of all of the potential issues and barriers that must be overcome to ensure the task is successful, and show how these problems can be dealt with in the best way. You will normally use the other members of your class as participants in your training programme.

As you can see from the above list of modules; whether you are taking Level 1, 2, 3 or even the Advanced Diploma, there are a huge range of college units which will fully prepare you for life as a social worker. The above modules are just the tip of the iceberg, there are so many more fascinating and helpful topics to choose from.

In the next chapter, we will provide you with a detailed insight into the life of a student studying social work at university. We will take you from your initial interview, to undergraduate and then postgraduate training; to ensure that you have all of the knowledge needed to make a success of yourself on a university course.

CHAPTER 4

University

A social work degree will help you to develop important knowledge and understanding of the key areas within the social sector. Your degree will place a fundamental emphasis on topics such as law and professional principles, and will ultimately provide you with the theoretical and practical knowledge required to gain a job within the social sector. You will learn how to make professional judgements, apply a range of interventional techniques and gain a valuable insight into human rights, social justice, diversity and equality. Furthermore, your communicational abilities and practice techniques will be noticeably enhanced. If you are someone looking to work within the social sector, then a university degree is the best way for you to train.

Once you have completed your A Levels or college course, you will be ready to apply. Providing you have met the relevant grades, a large portion of universities will invite you for an interview. This may seem slightly unusual, but the requirements for health and social care demand a very particular type of personality, and therefore it is important for a university to assess you prior to accepting your application. In the next section, we will guide you through potential interview questions and provide sample answers that will help to improve your chances of a successful interview. You can also refer back to the questions we covered in the previous topic, for further information. In chapter 8, you will find even more interview questions and answers, along with a list of top interview tips and tricks to help you with your interview technique.

UNIVERSITY INTERVIEW

Usually you will be invited to attend an interview with one of the lecturers from the course. This will take the form of a short, fairly informal chat, where you will discuss your expectations for the course and allow the interviewer to gage your personality and whether you are suitable for the course. The best way to prepare for this is to make sure that you have all of your answers ready in advance. If you come into the interview ready for the types of question that you will be asked, and know the answers you will give; you will come across as prepared and confident. Both of these factors will positively increase your chances of

Below you will find a list of potential questions and sample responses, which you might encounter in a university interview.

1. Why have you chosen social work?

This question is asked in order to test your knowledge of what the subject entails. Think carefully about your response, how is social work different from other caring related fields? Tell the interviewer about your desire to make a difference, and use any personal or work related experience to support your answer.

Write out your answer to this question in the box provided, and then compare it with the sample response below:

Sample response:

'I have chosen social work because I've always wanted to make a difference to peoples lives. Social work will provide me with the platform to do this. I took health and social care at both GCSE and A Level, and now I would love the opportunity to further my studies. Through work experience in a care home, and looking after my own Grandmother whilst she suffered from Alzheimer's, I already possess a wealth of knowledge and practical skills that would lend to my ability to succeed on this course. I've always been interested in helping people, and witnessing a close friend of mine deal with the effects of drug and alcohol abuse has only instilled in me a further desire to become a social worker. I really believe that your university is the best place to help me do this.'

2. What do you think are the most important values for a social worker?

This question is asking for two things. Firstly, they want to know that you understand the importance of social care values, and secondly (without directly asking) they want you to confirm that you meet with these values. Prior to your interview, look up the British Association of Social Workers, research their values/ethics and then make a list. Order this list in accordance of importance to you. Next to the top 3, write down why they are important to you. When it comes to answering this question, you don't have to list every single value, just make sure that you have 2 or 3 really important values that mean something to you. The interviewer just wants to know that you care, and that you are passionate about the subject.

Write out your answer to this question in the box provided, and then compare it with the sample response below:

Sample response:

'I personally have 3 values which I consider to be the most important. The first, is to treat each person as an individual and a whole. This is really important when working within social care, no two people are the same and every individual will have specific needs and requirements. It's fundamental as a social worker that you are able to recognise this and provide them with the best service that you can. Secondly, I will always challenge discrimination. As someone who wants to promote love, understanding and unity, I am against any principle which defies these. I will actively work to remove discrimination from both the workplace, and the public environment. Finally, I am a strong believer in promoting a trustworthy attitude to work. As a social worker, it is really important that you are an honest and reliable person, whom service users can rely upon. This will help you to build up a good working relationship with clients, and can only be beneficial for everyone involved. The more an individual can trust you, the better positioned you will be to help them.'

3. Can you describe a stressful experience that you have had, and how you dealt with it?

This is a fairly simple question. The best way to answer is to structure your response into three parts. Explain the issue, what you did to resolve it, and the end (positive) conclusion to the problem. You can use either personal or work based examples here, to show that you have past practical experience in dealing with the type of scenarios you will encounter as a social worker. The worst thing you can say here is, 'I don't get stressed'. This shows a lack of understanding and sensitivity; the asker wants to know that you can identify particular stressful situations and deal with them effectively.

Write out your answer to this question in the box provided, and then compare it with the sample response below:

Sample response:

'Whilst working at a care home I experienced stressful situations on a daily basis. One occasion I can remember was when an elderly resident vanished from the premises. Everyone was panicking, and couldn't find her. I joined the search and located her at the end of the care garden. She was confused and hiding behind the shed. I slowly coaxed her out, relaxed her and made sure she knew I was trustworthy. I then guided her back to the house. I made sure she was kept warm after being outside in the cold, fetched her a hot drink and helped her prepare for bed. On a personal level, I know that as a result of helping my own Grandmother with her Alzheimer's, I am far more prepared to deal with emotionally challenging situations. I can keep a cool head in these scenarios, and make calm and reasoned judgements.'

4.   Do you have any prejudices?

This is a tough question. For most people, the immediate answer would simply be, 'no.' While there is nothing wrong with that response, you should remember that prejudice can cover a wide variety of topics. Perhaps there is a particular character trait or characteristic that you make an assumption about, which makes you behave differently. If you are honest, and tell the interviewer about how you are working to change or remove your prejudice, you will come across better as a result. This will show both strength of character and self-awareness, each of which are important tools for any social worker.

Write out your answer to this question in the box provided, and then compare it with the sample response below:

Bury College
Millennium LRC

Sample response:

'I would say that I can sometimes be prejudiced against people who drink too much. This is a result of a family history with alcohol. I'm working extremely hard to change my views though, and have previously volunteered to help at organisations such as Alcoholics Anonymous. As a social worker, I know that it's really important to be fair and non-discriminatory against all people, regardless of their circumstances; and therefore I'm doing my utmost to better my own beliefs.'

5. Can you give an example of when you have taken action to counter discrimination or oppression?

This is a very common interview question, and is easily answered. Similarly to question 3, you should structure your response into three parts. What was the issue, how was it dealt with and what was the end result?

Write out your answer to this question in the box provided, and then compare it with the sample response below.

Sample response:

'My mother is a teacher at a local school. In order to aid my development as a social worker, I took a period of work experience helping out in her classes. She teaches children from ages 7-9. During my time assisting, I noticed that a group of the children were mocking another student for the colour of his skin. I immediately stepped in, separated the two parties and informed the offenders that their actions were wrong. I took steps to educate the children on how their behaviour was offensive and discriminatory and made them apologise to the boy. I also informed my mother, who wrote to the offending student's parents to inform them of their children's attitude. The parents consequently made sure that their children understood the gravity of their behaviour, and from then on there were no more issues.'

6. Can you describe an example of when you have worked effectively as a member of a team?

As a social worker, you will frequently be working as part of a wider team to help service users. Therefore, you need to have good team working skills. Similarly to the previous question, structure the answer into issue, response and end result.

Write out your answer to this question in the box provided, and then compare it with the sample response below.

Sample response:

'*I recently volunteered to work with a new member of our team at work. The task required us to successfully complete a stock-take of the entire warehouse within a short timeframe. The reason why I volunteered for the task is because I am a conscientious person who enjoys working with other people, and carrying out tasks to a high standard. Initially I showed the new team member how to stock-take in a professional manner in accordance with company guidelines. He had never carried out this type of work before and I wanted to ensure he was comfortable with the task, and that he was doing it correctly. Once I had achieved this we both then set about methodically working through each aisle, stocktaking as we went along. Periodically we would stop to ensure that the task was being done correctly. At the end of the specified timeframe, we had completed the stock-take and were able to provide accurate figures to our line manager. Whilst working as a team member, I always concentrate on effective communication, focusing on the task at hand and providing support to team members who require assistance.'*

7. Following this course, what are your career ambitions?

Try to be honest when answering this question. If you can, tell the interviewer about a specific area of the social sector in which you would like to work. If you can't, however, don't worry. It's okay to tell the interviewer that you are hoping the course will help you to decide; and that you are interested in gaining experience in as many areas as possible prior to making a career choice. They just want to know that they are taking on someone who is interested in pursuing the course beyond degree level. You could also tell the interviewer that you are hoping to take the course to postgraduate too; as this will show ambition and a desire to continue developing your education. Research the university and the course, so that you can show some prior knowledge of how the course will help you develop as a social worker.

Write out your answer to this question in the box provided, and then compare it with the sample response below.

Sample response:

'Well, I'm very interested in both childcare and helping the elderly. I've spent lots of time working in a care home, and babysitting for friends, neighbours and family; so I've got a wealth of experience in both areas. Having said that, I haven't made a definitive career decision yet, and I'm hoping that your course will help me to decide which option I should take. I know you have lots of available modules, in a wide variety of topics, and I'm willing to give any of the modules a go. I'm always eager to take on new challenges.'

8. Do you have any questions for me?

This is a hugely important part of the interview process, and one where many candidates fail to impress. You should always aim to show the university that you are interested and enthusiastic in study-ing with them, and therefore the worst thing you can say here is 'I don't know'. Prior to the interview, prepare a list of 5 to 6 questions that you can ask in this situation. That way, even if one, two or three of your questions are covered by the information given to you during the interview, you will still be prepared with more. Questions can include the following:

- What marks will I need to progress to postgraduate? What is the selection process?

- How much of the learning time will be spent in a practical-ly-based environment?

- How will the practical work be assessed?

- Can you suggest any useful reading that will enhance my skills, prior to beginning the course?

- How many hours of study per week does the programme involve?

- How long will it normally take to make a decision on my application?

UNDERGRADUATE MODULES

Once you have been accepted, you will begin your undergraduate degree. The type of modules that you will take at undergraduate, will depend largely on the institution to which you are applying. Universities will differ in their approach, with some favouring certain modules over others. However, the one thing that all university courses guarantee for candidates who finish their undergraduate course, is a wider knowledge of the social sector. On almost every single course, you will spend a significant portion of your time in a work place environment, gaining practical experience. We have conducted detailed research, and produced a comprehensive list of the type of modules you could expect to find at undergraduate level. We hope this gives you a broader idea of what to look out for during your initial 3 years at university. You might encounter any of the following modules at any point during your initial 3 years, and they are just a few of many hundreds of possible available options.

SOCIAL WORK AND DRUGS:

This module aims to give students an understanding of how social workers can deal with service users who are having problems with drugs, the use of drugs in society and harm prevention. The unit will examine and evaluate the effectiveness of the various services that are available to drug users within society, and how discrimination can negatively affect people. Finally, the module will examine the legalities of social work practice in a relation to drug taking service users.

MENTAL HEALTH:

This module aims to give students an understanding of the nature of mental health services. It will include a broad examination of legislative issues, social work policies and practice techniques. The unit will explore the perception of mental health in society, alternative treatments and techniques, and the way in which social workers can aid service users who are suffering from mental health issues.

RESEARCH:

This module aims to give students a wider understanding of the importance of research whilst working within the social sector. The unit will explore data collection techniques, methods of interpreting data and the advantages and disadvantages of various forms of research. The module will also explore the way in which legal practice and policies can affect research, both positively and negatively.

FAMILY SOCIAL CARE:

This module will provide students with a wider understanding of family and child protection based social work. It will demonstrate different methods of safeguarding children and engaging with families, whilst balancing the interests of different members of the family. The unit will study intervention methods that can be used to prevent the breakdown of families, demonstrate care planning and explore case reviews.

ADULT SOCIAL CARE:

This module will provide students with a good knowledge of the way in which social workers can impact the lives of disabled, or older service users. The unit will explore the social principles which help workers within the sector to deliver support, guidance and assistance to those who need it. Finally, students will be given an insight into the interview and decision making skills needed to assess individuals capability to depend on themselves.

CONTEMPORARY SOCIAL CARE:

This module will examine issues in modern social care, and explore why said issues have become serious problems. The unit will explore the way in which social issues are a direct consequence of economic or social deficiencies, and how they can be effected by the welfare ideologies of the community. Students will explore issues such as poverty, social justice, safeguarding, and gain an understanding into past, present and future issues that arise within the social care sector.

SOCIAL WORK AND YOUNG PEOPLE:

This module will focus exclusively on social care in relation to young people, with particular attention to young offenders. It will aim to demonstrate various different interventional methods that can be used to support young people, legalities and safeguarding. The module will also focus heavily on behavioural theory, reasons for certain types of behaviour, peer-to-peer relationships and the relationship between parent and child.

WORK BASED PLACEMENTS:

The number of work based placements you take on your course will depend on the institution that you are attending. It could be anywhere from 2 to 4 placements over the space of 3 years. Each placement will aim to show you different things about working within the sector; for example on your first placement, you might be tasked with helping in an elderly care home, whereas on your final placement, you will gain more experience in interview techniques, assessment procedures, data collection and recommendations. By the end of the final placement, you should be fully prepared to work within the social sector.

DISSERTATION:

In your final year, you will be asked to write a dissertation. This will require you to produce an extended essay, which explores a particular piece of literature or social-work related topic. In your dissertation, you will be expected to demonstrate an extended knowledge and understanding of all of the skills you have learned throughout your time at university. You will be expected to use a clear, analytical, rationale and practical examples to support your leading argument. Most courses will brief, coach and prepare their students for their dissertations well in advance of the start date for this submission.

POSTGRADUATE STUDY

Once you have finished your undergraduate degree, you might consider moving up to postgraduate level. The entry requirements are largely dependent upon the institution to which you are applying, but the majority will look for a 2:1 minimum. A postgraduate degree will provide you with a more advanced understanding of social work than you would receive at an undergraduate level, and will give you more challenging work placements. When it comes to applying for jobs, a postgraduate degree is a fantastic thing to include on your CV; as it shows a real commitment to the cause and a passion to excel within the field of social work.

Most postgraduate courses last for 2 years. Due to the nature of the course, most universities do not offer a 'part time' option, as candidates need to be wholly committed to the subject and will spend most of their time in work based placements. Candidates will need to pass every single module in the first year, in order to progress to the second year.

Below we have listed the typical format for a taught, full time post-graduate course. The modules that you take will depend upon the university to which you are applying.

YEAR 1

INTRODUCTION TO ADVANCED SOCIAL WORK:

This module will introduce students to the key principles and values which will be essential to the course. It will build on their previous experience to focus on service user perspectives and the skills and strategies needed to practice to the best standards. This unit will aim to prepare students for their first practice placement.

LIFE DEVELOPMENT:

This module will engage students in critical theory in relation to child and adult development. It will look at the ways in which social work develops and changes according to the stage of life of the service user, types of research and interventional methods. The module will help students to develop their assessment making ability based on the age of service users and explore national context and paternal relationships.

SOCIAL LEGALITIES:

This module will explore the laws and social policies of England. It will examine the English legal system, human rights and young offenders. Using case reviews, students will gain a detailed under-standing of their statutory rights as a social worker and the legal barriers that they might face while performing the role. The unit will also explore the portrayal of social work in the media and the affect that this has on public perception.

PLACEMENT 1:

For their initial placement, students will be given up to 90 days in a work based setting, to practice the skills that they have learned from their modules so far. This period usually includes a number of preparatory workshops and development days beforehand, so that students are ready for the challenges they will face during the time spent in their placement.

YEAR 2

INTERVENTIONAL METHODS:

In the first module of the second year, students will study a number of theoretical interventional techniques, and learn how to apply these in real life practice. They will be required to demonstrate how they have used initial interventional techniques and methods in their prior work placement. The module will explore critical situational awareness and highlight the advantages and disadvantages of different practical methods. It should also begin to develop a knowledge of the specialist pathways that are available following postgraduate study.

SOCIAL SAFEGUARDING:

In this module, students will further develop their ability to plan, evaluate and intervene on behalf of vulnerable children and adults. The unit will examine topics such as mental health, domestic abuse, substance abuse, disability and elderly care. Students will require a strong ability to perform risk assessment on children and adults, in order to critically evaluate situations in the correct manner and to operate within the confinements of the law.

PLACEMENT 2:

The final placement on the course can last up to 120 days, and will take place in a different setting to that of the first. The setting will test the knowledge that students have learned in their second year modules, help them to understand the reality of social work practice, and challenge their ability to work with service user groups that they might not be familiar with. Usually, students will work within a placement that relates to their intended career trajectory.

DISSERTATION:

Finally, students will have to complete a dissertation. This should consist of a detailed study of a topic relevant to social work; and should allow them to incorporate all of the knowledge and skills that they have learned into a literary, research and review essay.

Once you have finished your postgraduate studies, you will be ready to move on into the world of work. Over the next few chapters, we will explore some of the most popular options available for you as a social worker. We will show you how to prepare for interviews, how to craft your CV and Covering Letter; and even provide you with day in the life segments of real social workers.

CHAPTER 5

Career Change

If you are someone who has been out of education for a long time, or employed in another field altogether, you might be wondering how you would go about making the switch. In the next section we will show you the steps needed to do this.

For many people, a switch to social work is determined by their desire to help other people. You might be feeling as if you want to make a difference to the community, or give something back. This is highly admirable, but it's also important to recognise that social work is not for everyone. Social work is an emotionally draining role, which takes great perseverance and courage. You'll need to be organised, patient and caring with everyone you meet, and will often find yourself dealing with extremely difficult situations. It is highly important that you are psychologically equipped to handle the challenges of the role. If you are sure that this is the right position for you, then below we have provided you with detailed advice on how you can go about making the switch.

QUALIFICATIONS

If you are looking to make a career switch to social work, you will need both experience and qualifications. Social work is a graduate profession, and therefore you'll need either an honours or postgraduate degree from a HCPC recognised course. In order to achieve this, you'll need experience. As we have identified in our previous chapter on university courses, course providers look for candidates to have spent a certain amount of time working in the field before accepting them. This is to ensure that you are fully prepared for the nature of the work. University courses do not want candidates who will drop out in the middle of the year, when they realise the work is too hard for them. They need students who are in it for the long haul. There are plenty of ways you can gain this experience, as we will outline below.

WORK EXPERIENCE

Gaining work experience in the social sector is a great way to boost your chances of employment, or being accepted onto a university course. The best places to look for this experience are:

-**Voluntary organisations and projects.** In the UK, there are a huge variety of voluntary projects set up to aid vulnerable people. These organisations are always looking for new recruits, who care about helping others. A quick google search should bring up a list of local or national organisations. Make sure that when you are applying for these organisations, you study the volunteer specification carefully. Some voluntary organisations will ask for prior experience before signing up to them. If you are just starting in the industry, you need an organisation that will accept you as a beginner. You might also be expected to attend an initial interview with the organisation before starting voluntary work with them. This will usually take the form of an informal chat, so that the organisation can assess whether you have the right personality for their organisation, and whether you are a caring, genuine person. In chapter 8 of this guide, we've covered a wide range of social worker interview questions. You can use these, as well as the college and university interview questions that we have already provided you, as a basic outline for the type of things you might be asked. If you are someone who really cares about helping people, you should not be intimidated by this process. Voluntary organisations are simply looking for candidates who share their ethics, values and care towards others. A great way to find local voluntary organisations is to contact your volunteer bureau, http://www.ncvo.org.uk/ncvo-volunteering

-**Local institutions.** You don't necessarily have to contact a voluntary organisation to gain experience in the field, there are a variety of local institutions that are likely to at least meet you to discuss voluntary work. Contact your nearest residential home and ask them if they need unpaid assistance, do the same for hospitals, nurseries or schools. While you might not experience success with every single organisation that you contact, if you can persuade someone that you are a helpful and caring person, they will be grateful for any unpaid help that you can offer. If you know someone who works in an institution, ask them to put in a good word. Don't be afraid to put yourself out there.

-Entry level College. There is no age limit on who can apply for college courses. Although it might take a longer period of time, you can enter at Level 1 Health and Social Care with a bare minimum of experience, and then progress up to Level 4. This will provide you with both qualifications and great experience.

TRANSFERABLE SKILLS

If you have come from another career, then you will inevitably have picked up new skills along the way. Some of these skills can be extremely useful for social workers. This includes:

- Problem solving skills.

- Communication and listening skills.

- Organisational skills.

- Mediation skills.

- A knowledge and understanding of law and legal procedures.

If you are passionate about making a career switch, you can do it. It doesn't matter if you are completely new to the industry, or have spent significant time working in another career. With the right experience, hard work and attitude, you can achieve exactly the same as any other person who started social work during their education. Your lack of experience is only a disadvantage if you don't address it. If you take active steps to gain the right level of experience, and demonstrate your competency in all of the required traits, you have as much chance of becoming a social worker as anyone else. Believe in yourself, and you can do anything that you set your mind to.

CHAPTER 6

Application Form

ve completed your studies, it is time to look for work. ...g you will need to do is to register as a member of ...and Care Professions Council (HCPC). As a registered memb... the HCPC, you will attend regular training courses and assessment centres to update your methods and maintain your professional learning development. You will need to re-register with the HCPC every 3 years, and may be required to complete even further training in order to do so. While independent organisations may allow their employees to work before registering with the HCPC, local authorities are likely to reject anybody who is not registered with the HCPC prior to their application.

As a registered member of the HCPC, there are many organisations you can apply to. These include:

- Charities.
- Voluntary Agencies.
- Care Homes.
- Prisons.
- The NHS.
- Mental Health Groups.

If you are someone who has not yet decided which area they would like to specialise in, you can use a social work agency to find vacancies. A social work agency is a recruitment company which specialises in social work, and matches social workers looking for suitable positions. You would normally take a short-term contract which would provide you with a wide range of jobs and responsibilities. This will allow you to make an informed decision on which area of social work suits you best. The disadvantage of this system is that you may find it more difficult to make a significant impact, or exert your influence on the area in which you are posted. Typically, social workers can earn from £20,000 to £40,000, depending on their experience and qualifications. Senior managers in social work can earn up to £70,000, and some even earn more than this.

After you have registered with the HCPC, you need to craft a CV and Covering Letter. These will highlight all of your best qualities and make you stand out to potential employers. Social workers can be employed by a huge range of organisations, such as: hospitals, schools, police departments, government agencies, nursing homes and international organisations. A quick google search will bring up a huge number of roles for which you can apply. If you are applying to a local authority, you will most likely have to fill in an application form; whereas other employers will only require you to send in a CV and Covering Letter. In this chapter, we'll cover how to fill in an application form.

APPLICATION FORM:

When filling in application forms, you need to make sure that your qualities match up with the core competencies of the job, and the personal qualities listed in the advert. Both of these should be fairly simple to find, but are absolutely crucial when it comes to filling in your form. As a reminder, let's run through the core competencies that you will need to work as a social worker:

IDENTIFY AS A SOCIAL WORKER AND CONDUCT YOURSELF APPROPRIATELY

As a social worker, it's really important that you can conduct yourself in an appropriate manner. You need to work as an advocate for social work when meeting with clients, who are putting their trust in you. You need to conduct yourself within the standards set out by the British Association of Social Workers (BASW). You'll also need to recognise that as a social worker, you are responsible for improving your own practice. You need to engage yourself in learning and bettering yourself, taking courses, reflecting upon your own performance and developing methods that you can improve.

APPLY SOCIAL WORK ETHICS AND VALUES TO YOUR PROFESSIONAL PRACTICE

Ethics and professional values are a core element of being a social worker, and you need to demonstrate that you meet with and believe in the accepted standards. All of your decisions should be ethical, unbiased and well thought out according to the standards set out by the BASW, and the International Federation of Social Workers. You need to be someone who can respect and tolerate diversity and ambiguity when dealing with conflicts, and must be able to use ethical reasoning to resolve conflicts and difficult situations.

USE AND APPLY CRITICAL THINKING WHEN MAKING JUDGEMENTS

Decision making is key to the role of a social worker, and to make good decisions you need to be able to apply critical thinking. You'll need to demonstrate a full understanding of behavioural theory and learning methods, in order to show that you have taken every aspect into account before making reasoned judgements. You need to be able to identify the strengths and weaknesses of multiple sources of information, undertake research and lead various assessments. Finally, you'll need to demonstrate your ability to communicate both orally and in writing whilst working with service users, their relatives and other organisations.

RECOGNISE AND ACCEPT DIVERSITY

Social workers deal with a wide range of people, and therefore it's hugely important that you are someone who is able to recognise and accept diversity in the workplace. You'll need to recognise the impact that certain elements can have on culture and society, and will be expected to work in an unbiased manner with diverse groups of people. Often, this will test your communicational skills. It's important to recognise the way that people from different cultures will react to different things, and take this into account when you are working with these people.

UTILISE RESEARCH INFORMED PRACTICE

Research is extremely important for social workers in gaining all of the information they need to make judgements and assessments. It is only when you have made your assessment, that you can put the theories learned into practice. As a social worker you need to be constantly developing and improving new research techniques and methods, which will help you to provide the best service to your clients.

UTILISE BEHAVIOURAL KNOWLEDGE

As a social worker, you will be in constant contact with people. When dealing with these people, you will need to apply an advanced knowledge of behavioural theory to enhance your evaluations and assessments. This knowledge will be critical when used as evidence for/against decisions, and can often be the difference maker when it comes to devising solutions or interventions.

ENGAGE IN ASSESSMENTS, INTERVENTIONS AND EVALUATIONS WITH INDIVIDUALS, THEIR FAMILIES AND OTHER ORGANISATIONS

This is one of the most fundamental aspects of social work. As a social worker, you need to be able to engage in a wide variety of activities with individuals, their families and other connected organisations. This includes producing detailed and well researched interventional plans that are mutually agreed between all involved parties, collecting organising and interpreting data, negotiating and mediating with clients and developing further strategies for aiding and assisting service users.

After you have read through the above list, study the below information. The information is from a mock job description. Read it through carefully:

SMITH COUNCIL - JOB PROFILE

OCCUPATION	Social Worker
DEPARTMENT	Adult Social Care
RESPONSIBLE TO	Social Work Manager
GRADE	SW2

1. JOB DESCRIPTION

The purpose of the role is to deliver a highly effective service to disabled adults, undertake responsibility for working with particular cases in a supervised framework, and meet the needs of individual service users. The post holder will uphold the codes of conduct laid out by Smith Council, the HCPC and the College of Social Work.

The post holder will need to work with vulnerable adults, families and carers to ensure that their needs are met. They will need to assess, plan and implement safeguarding measures to ensure that all clients have equal opportunities. They will need to submit reports and assessments and work as part of a team to provide a good service to all of those involved.

2. PERSON SPECIFICATION

Essential Qualifications

- Registration with HCPC.

- Current enhanced DBS.

- A relevant qualification in Social Work, for example: a degree, a diploma or equivalent.

- A clean, full UK driving license.

Essential Experience

- Must be able to demonstrate experience of working within the social sector and an understanding of adult protection and mental capacity.

- Must have knowledge and experience with legislation, statutory rights and adult social care procedures.

- Must have knowledge and experience with practice models, research and psychological development theories.

Essential Skills

- ICT skills including a competent knowledge of Word, Power-Point and Excel.

- Strong communicational ability, both written and verbally, in order to present reports to a high standard.

- High quality of assessment skills, to ensure appropriate outcome for service users.

- Ability to work one-to-one with service users, families and carers.

- Ability to research evidence and apply theory when necessary.

- Ability to work within the boundaries of statutory requirements and guidance, social care policies, professional practice, ethics and legislation.

Essential Personal Qualities

- Must be able to engage with vulnerable adults, their families and carers.

- Must be able to build and develop working professional relationships with other social workers within the field, and the organisations that they work for. Post holder must be able to work with both voluntary and private agencies to obtain and share information, to benefit the overall decision making process.

- Must be someone who can be held accountable for their actions, with good levels of professional judgement. Furthermore, they must be able to make key decisions both on their own, and with the help of senior staff.

- Must be someone who is open to providing information, counselling and support to service users and carers.

- Must be someone with the ability to analyse and interpret personal data and information, and develop long term interventional strategies.

- Must be someone with well-developed communicational abilities, who can present sensitive information to a wide range of people.

Interviews will be held at the Smith Centre, Smithtown, ME98 12A, on the 31st June 2015. **For more information please contact 01622 123456**

THE APPLICATION FORM

Now that you have seen an example of what an online job description might look like, let's look at the application form itself. For the above job, you might expect to see something like this:

Title:

First Name

Surname:

DOB:

National Insurance Number:

Address:

Town or City:

County:

Postcode:

Country:

Landline Number:

Mobile Number:

Email Address:

1. Can you provide the relevant evidence that you are legally allowed to work in the UK?

   Yes/No

2. Can you provide the original of one of the following: a British passport, a UK residence permit or a legal document which proves that you are able to work in the UK?

   Yes/No

3. Do you require a work permit to be employed in the UK?

   Yes/No

4. If you were successful when is the earliest date that you could begin employment?

5. Are you a current employee of Smith Council?

    Yes/No

6. Are you related to or in a relationship with any elected member or officer of the council?

    Yes/No

Following all of this, you'll be asked to fill in your previous employment and educational history, as well as completing a disability act form. You'll also be required to provide references. Finally, you'll move onto the supporting statement.

SUPPORTING STATEMENT

This is the most important part of the application stage. While your educational and employment records carry significant weight, your supporting statement will be the best indication for the employer as to whether you are a suitable candidate. You will normally be given a statement that reads:

'Please outline why you believe that you are suitable for the selected role. Base your answer on the requirements given in the person specification. Failure to link your statement with each part of the person specification will likely lead to an unsuccessful application.'

Prior to answering this, read through the person specification again, and then make a list of all of the qualities the role requires. You should have noted down the following necessary person requirements:

•   Good communicational skills.

•   Good decision making, interpretation and assessment skills.

•   Good knowledge of legislation and ethical requirements.

•   Good presentational skills.

- Good knowledge of theoretical frameworks.

- Relatable, caring and friendly persona.

- Extensive experience of working with disabled adults, families and carers.

Now, craft these requirements into an acceptable response to the question. This is great practice for you if you ever have to write a covering letter or personal statement. Don't just list the requirements, give examples of how you have demonstrated the qualities that they are looking for. Remember that you are showing your key skills to the reader. Make sure you make a good first impression.

'Please outline why you believe that you are suitable for the selected role. Base your answer on the requirements given in the person specification. Failure to link your statement with each part of the person specification will likely lead to an unsuccessful application.'

Sample response:

'I believe that I am perfect for this position. Firstly, I've got fantastic communicational abilities. I've demonstrated this on many occasions, most recently when I undertook a practical placement for my postgraduate course in social work. I was placed in a hospital, assisting in the social support team. This often involved dealing with the families of bereaved relatives, and was particularly challenging. I used my communicational abilities to help the families in question and created a positive relationship. While working at the hospital, I also gained experience in dealing with elderly patients. On one particular occasion, I had to help the senior team come to a decision on whether a patient would be better placed in a care residence than in his own home. We interviewed the subject and then presented our findings back to the group. This was a really helpful exercise and allowed me to demonstrate my great presentational and decision making skills. It also gave me experience in communicating and building a rapport with a service user who had difficulty in expressing himself. My postgraduate studies have provided me with detailed knowledge of the legal necessities that a role such as this would demand. I'm a caring, relatable person who loves helping other members of the community, and I think this would be a fantastic opportunity for me. I'd make a great addition to your team, and I hope you'll consider me for the role.'

As you can see, we have combined our experience with the skills and qualities that the position is looking for, in order to create a strong and concise response. Make sure you let the organisation in question know that you would love to work for them, and that you are a great team player. Look at the way that we have addressed some of the core competencies in our response. We've shown that we've got great communicational skills, assessment and decision making ability, mediation skills and interpersonal ability. Combined with our experience, this makes us seem ideal for the role.

TIPS FOR FILLING IN YOUR APPLICATION FORM

• Make sure you read the whole application form before preparing your response, including the guidance notes.

• Read and understand the personal specification and the core competencies of social work.

• Try to tailor your answers around the core competencies, and include any keywords or phrases that you think are relevant.

• Make sure that you base your answers on actual events that you have experienced in either your work or personal life.

• Make sure you keep a photocopy of your completed application form prior to sending it off. You could be asked questions related to it during the interview stage.

• Get someone else to read through your completed application form to check for spelling and grammar mistakes.

• Pay attention to your handwriting, spelling, punctuation and grammar. Remember that this is a formal application, so the use of jargon and slang is unacceptable. Good written communicational is essential for social workers.

If your application form is successful, you will receive an email inviting you to attend an interview. In chapter 8, we will cover a wide range of interview tips and tricks, to help you through this process. In the next section, we'll look at how to apply for social work roles using a Covering Letter and CV.

CHAPTER 7
CV and Cover Letter

If you are applying for an organisation that does not require you to fill in an application form, you'll need to devise a Covering Letter and CV. Much like the application form, these should tell the employer about your personal qualities, qualifications and experience. You should begin with the Covering Letter.

COVERING LETTER

A Covering Letter serves as a written introduction to your resume (CV), and helps the employer get to know you on a more personal level. In your Covering Letter, you should include your skills and interests, why you are applying for the role, and your future ambitions. If you have any past work experience, this is also a great thing to include. This is very similar to the supporting statement from the application form. If you are applying to a role with an available person specification, then you can base your attributes around that. You should always tailor your Covering Letter and CV to the role that you are applying for. If there is limited information on the role, then you should cover a wide spectrum of qualities.

Study the mock person specification below, and then write up a Covering Letter for the job in the box provided. Compare it with the Covering Letter that we have provided.

EXAMPLE

Our client currently has a job vacancy for a social worker to work for a child care team in Smithtown. This vacancy has an initial 3 month contract and the pay rate for this role is up to £18 per hour.

Duties include:

• Contributing to the development of ongoing initiatives.

• Working with voluntary and private agencies.

• Advising, counselling and supporting clients in individual and group settings.

- Recruiting, assessing, and supporting adoptive and foster carers in order to ensure the best service for the child.

Requirements: All applicants must be registered with HCPC, and have a recognised qualification in social work, as well as related work experience.

Before writing out your cover letter, study the above information in detail. What do you think are the core competencies that this job is looking for in an applicant? Take each of the duties and assign a competency to it.

'Contributing to the development of ongoing initiatives'

Depending on the nature of the ongoing projects, this indicates that you'll need to work as part of a team and adapt quickly to already existing projects.

'Working with voluntary and private agencies'

This means that you'll need to use your communicational and organisational skills to conduct meetings with other involved organisations, in order to solve issues.

'Advising, counselling and supporting clients in individual and group settings'

This means that you'll need to have a great grasp of behavioural theory, mediation and negotiation methods, as well as knowledge of how to handle larger groups of people compared to just one individual. You'll have to identify the need for specific behaviour in specific situations, and then utilise this according to the requirements.

'Recruiting, assessing, and supporting adoptive and foster carers in order to ensure the best service for the child.'

In order to do this, you'll need to demonstrate fantastic judgement and assessment skills, as well as communicational ability. You'll need to have a wide knowledge of assessment and research methods, in order to produce conclusive evidence for or against the case of selected foster parents.

From the four short lines above, you can already see how your competency is being tested. This should give you some idea of how to break down a job description, and select the key words which are most important to the applicant. Using this information, create your own cover letter in the box below.

Sample Cover Letter

Dear Sir/Madam,

I am writing to apply for the position of Social Child Care Worker. I believe that I am a fantastic candidate for this role, and meet all of the criteria listed. I'm a really caring and empathetic person, with a strong background in social work. I've always been interested in childcare, and from as early as 14 years old, I babysat for my friends, neighbours and family. I also took various childcare modules at GCSE, A Level and University level. During my undergraduate degree, I took a placement working with young children in a home. This was an extremely rewarding experience and taught me a great deal about the value of childcare. Following this, I moved on to take a postgraduate degree. For my initial placement, I spent time working with young children in a juvenile detention centre; before moving on to complete a secondary placement within the paediatric ward of my local hospital. This has provided me with fantastic knowledge and experience of dealing with young people. I built up great working relationships with all of the staff and people that I met during my placements, and this was down to my friendly and relatable approach. I am someone with high career ambitions to specialise in childcare, and I believe this would be an incredible opportunity for me to improve upon the skills that I already possess. I am a responsible and hardworking individual who is passionate about making a difference to the lives of younger people, and I would appreciate it if you could consider me for this position.

As you can see in the above response, we have presented ourselves as someone who is a great fit for the role. Highlighting your previous experience is a fantastic way to do this. The majority of candidates will simply list qualities that they have, without actually providing evidence or examples. If you can link your experience and skills with the qualities listed in the person and job description; you will greatly increase your chances of success.

Of course, no Covering Letter is complete without a CV. Now, we will draft a mock social worker resume, so that you can get a good idea of the way in which you should present yourself to potential employers. For the purpose of this exercise, we will tailor our CV to meet the requirements of the job listed above.

Generally, when you submit a CV, you should keep it to a length of 2 pages maximum. In our example CV, we have elaborated in more detail during the 'work experience' section. This is to provide you with a wider understanding of the various types of experience you might choose to include, how you can use the experience to benefit your application, and how you can present it to your employer. Don't use all of your experience. When you write your own application, try to trim the information down, so that you have only used information that is relevant and specific to the job itself.

EXAMPLE CV

Gwendoline Brown
Smith Street
Smith Town
Smithshire
Tel: 01634 123456
Email: GwenBrown@emailaddresshere.com

Personal profile:

I am an experienced, caring and compassionate social worker who has recently finished her postgraduate degree. At the conclusion of these studies, I registered as a member of the HCPC. I've always wanted to make a difference to the community, and there is no better way to do this than to aid those who are the most vulnerable of all, children.

From early on, I tailored my studies so that they would fit into the childcare spectrum. I took childcare modules at both GCSE and A Level, and then during my degree I worked in several child and youth-based placements. These included working in a children's home, assisting at a juvenile detention centre and being a junior member of the social paediatric team at my local hospital.

All of this has given me vital experience of dealing with children and young people, and now I would love the opportunity to take a full time position. I consider no job too big, and would relish the challenge of working for your organisation.

ACADEMIC EXPERIENCE:

Smith School:

GCSE Maths: B

GCSE English: A

GCSE History: B

GCSE Health and Social Care: A

AS Level Health and Social Care: A

A-Level Health and Social Care: A

Smith University:

BA Social Work, 2:1

MA Social Work: Merit.

PREVIOUS EMPLOYMENT HISTORY, DATES AND DUTIES:

Ongoing: 100+ hour experience of babysitting for friends, neighbours and family.

This position involves watching and caring for young children whilst their guardians are out, feeding them and putting them to bed.

12//03/2008-17/03/2008: 1 week of work experience assisting at Smith day-care/nursery. This position involved working with those in charge, as part of a team, to ensure the wellbeing and safety of young attendees. Activities included: creating a fun and friendly atmosphere for the children, participating in group singing exercises and helping to put children down for naps. This position also involved communicating with parents who were dropping off/ collecting or assisting with the playgroup activities.

14/10/2008-24/10/2008: 2 weeks of work experience assisting student services at Smith elementary school.

This position involved working with student services to provide a support base for children under the age of 11. The initial week was spent shadowing those in charge, before assisting in the second week. Activities included: meeting in a team setting with students to rectify their behaviour, meeting students one-to-one to discuss behavioural changes, and submitting reviews/reports on particular students. The position required me to understand and apply large amounts of behavioural theory.

25/11/2009-01/12/2009: 1 week of work experience in Smith residential home.

This position involved working in an elderly care home, to provide support services to the residents. Activities included: helping residents with personal tasks, leading reading and writing groups, organising group activities and entertainment, and generally assisting residents with everyday life. The position also required great communication between myself, the service users and their relatives.

04/02/2011-17/06/2011: 4 month placement in Ficshire Children's Home.

This position involved working as a junior social worker in a children's home, to assist senior members of staff in dealing with the residents. Activities included: providing a support service to young people, cooking, cleaning, organising day trips and activities, producing and reviewing file cases, communicating with foster parents and building up a trust with the children. This was a fantastic experience, and I developed great relationships with everyone involved; many of whom I am still in contact with today.

10/10/2011-15/12/2011: 2 month placement at How2Helpp.

This position involved working in a voluntary organisation, dealing with troubled service users. The work was emotionally challenging and I encountered a wide range of issues, including alcoholism and drug abuse. I was required to apply large amounts of behavioural and interventional theory, in order to assist the users involved. For a small part of this placement, I also worked in the How2Helpp charity shop.

03/03/2012-10/05/2012: 2 month placement at Ficshire Women's refuge.

This position involved working alongside senior staff at a women's refuge, to provide support and care to victims of domestic violence. Ficshire Women's refuge allowed service users to bring along relatives of the age of 12 and under, and therefore I also had to deal with younger children as well as the women themselves. This was a great experience as it gave me a wider understanding of family relationships; and how to deal with these issues as a social worker.

05/01/2013-05/07/2013: 6 month placement at Ficshire Juvenile Detention Centre.

This position involved working alongside senior staff and officers at a juvenile detention centre, dealing with young offenders. My duties included: taking part in behavioural therapy meetings, processing written reports and evaluations on young offenders, building a relationship with assigned offenders to try and establish behavioural changes, and submitting case evidence to appeal units for consideration of parole.

10/10/2013-11/05/2014: 7 month placement at Ficshire Hospital, Paediatric Ward.

This position involved working alongside the social team of Ficshire hospital, to provide support to patients on their paediatric ward. As a junior member of the team, I assisted in counselling relatives of patients, interviewing relatives and staff for assessment purposes, dealing directly with young patients, and providing care and support. I also led various projects and presentations. This was the biggest challenge of my current career, and it was a huge success.

KEY COMPETENCIES:

- I am registered as a member of the HCPC, and have a strong educational and practical background in social work.

- I am a highly relatable, compassionate and empathetic person with the ability to make safe and unbiased assessments.

- I have fantastic communicational and customer service abilities, as well as good organisational skills.

- I have a wealth of experience in dealing with vulnerable service users, particularly children.

- I have a great working knowledge of social behavioural theory, concepts and framework.

- I have a detailed knowledge of legislation and legal boundaries.

SIGNIFICANT ACHIEVEMENTS:

- Recently received a merit in my postgraduate studies and registered as a member of the HCPC.

- Built up great relationships with service users in both adult and child-based placements.

- Have successfully maintained my own babysitting service from a very young age.

- Successfully reviewed and implemented detailed changes to the behavioural plans of young offenders; with great results.

HOBBIES AND INTERESTS:

When I am not working, I spend most of my time socialising with friends and family. I love to keep fit, and was a member of various sports teams at both school and university. I'm also someone who is really interested in fashion, and I take great value in my own appearance. I regularly post on various online discussion forums.

SOCIAL WORKER CV TIPS

As you can see, in our CV we have demonstrated a wide range of qualities and experience. The practical nature of the industry means that it is hugely important for you to put across the **competency and experience** you can bring to the organisation. Study the way that our CV has demonstrated that we are in possession of the core competencies listed in the previous chapter. Don't just list the competencies, demonstrate with relevant examples that you understand them and have experience of carrying them out. Below we've included a list of top tips, which you can use when writing your own CV.

- Take the time to read the job description for the position you are applying for very carefully. Gain an understanding of the position you have applied for and read the key skills and qualities required in the role. We also recommend that you use a highlighter pen to highlight the key areas of the job before you write your CV.

• Make sure that your CV is no more than two sides in length. It should be concise, easy to read and free from waffle or irrelevance.

• At the beginning of your CV, create an introductory statement that says a little bit about you, what your experiences are and what you have to offer this particular post. This will immediately tell the person reading it that you are serious about their job. It will also demonstrate that you are not a 'serial' applicant who is only interested in getting a job, regardless of which company it is with.

• Insert keywords and phrases from the job description in your CV. The person reading your CV will pick up on these straight away and it will help them to identify that you should be short-listed for interview.

Using the above information, you should now have a clear idea of how to construct your CV and Covering Letter according to the requirements of the role. In the next chapter, we'll give you a wide range of potential interview questions that you might encounter if your application was successful; and provide you with sample responses to these questions.

CHAPTER 8

Interview

Once you have sent off your form, you will have to wait for a response from the organisation. This can sometimes take a long time, so be patient. Hopefully they will contact you to invite you to attend an interview. In order to pass this stage, you will need to be fully prepared. This chapter will cover a wide range of potential interview questions, and show you some great ways to answer these questions. At the end of the chapter, we'll provide you with some useful interview tips and tricks, to help you prepare yourself beforehand.

While there are some questions that you should expect to encounter in any social work based interview; many of the questions asked will depend upon the role to which you are applying. The majority of social workers tend to specialise either in supporting children and families, or working with vulnerable adults. With this in mind, we will provide you with both general and specialist answers to interview questions that you are likely to be asked in an interview.

INTERVIEW QUESTIONS

1.   Tell me about yourself.

This is a commonly used icebreaker, which helps to build up an initial rapport between you and the interviewer. It gives you the opportunity to talk about yourself, your interests and your background. The key to answering this question is to structure your response in a clear and concise manner. Start with your GCSE's or early qualifications, then include any key work experience. Finally, discuss your most recent accomplishments. Structuring your response will ensure that the interviewer gets a clear idea of who you are and how your background will help you to perform the role.

Using the above information, write your answer to this question in the box provided, and then compare it with the sample response below.

Sample response:

'I'm a really caring and compassionate person, who has always been interested in social work and looking after children. I started my own babysitting service at a very young age, and then pursued this interest at both GCSE and A Level. As part of the placements on my undergraduate course, I worked in a children's home. This was the most rewarding experience of my career. I developed fantastic relationships with all of the children involved and am still in contact with many of them now. After my undergraduate degree, I studied social work at postgraduate level, and took placements in a juvenile detention centre and on the paediatric social team within a hospital. Both of these roles challenged me to my utmost, but I ultimately emerged a more capable, experienced and confident social worker. I'm extremely grateful for the opportunities that I have been afforded. I'm now looking for a role which allows me to use the skills I've developed.'

2. What do you know about our organisation?

This is another commonly asked question. Here, the interviewer wants to know that you have done your research on their company prior to the interview. You don't have to know the organisation inside out, but you should always make sure that you have a good idea of the services they offer, when they started, how successful they are, any recent awards they have been nominated for, and their company values. If you can't answer this question then you will come across as uninterested or unenthusiastic. Obviously, your answer will be specific to the company to which you are applying. If you haven't got a particular job in mind, just google any social work vacancy. Find out the name of the employer and then research them. Use this information to structure your answer, and don't be afraid to flatter the employer either.

Sample response:

'I know that you are a highly influential voluntary organisation, who have made a huge impact within the UK. You were founded in 2006 and provide support to vulnerable adults on a variety of issues; such as alcohol, drugs and mental health. One of the things that drew me to this organisation was your recent nomination for the HCAM

award, which recognises contributions to health, care and medical services in the United Kingdom. I'm someone who really cares about making a positive difference to people's lives, and I know that this is a value that your organisation shares and delivers upon, on a daily basis.'

3. What are your biggest strengths?

This is a great question for you, as it allows you to highlight your best qualities. Make sure that your answer is relevant to the role. As we have mentioned several times, personality is extremely important within the social sector. It's a difficult and often emotionally challenging career, and therefore the organisation needs to know that they are hiring someone who can deliver on their personal expectations. As we have relayed at several points in this book, a good social worker is someone who is:

- Caring and non-judgemental.
- Organised.
- Able to make key decisions.
- An excellent communicator.

In your answer, show the interviewer that you are in possession of the personal qualities that they are looking for, and that you know how they are relevant to the role.

Sample response:

'My biggest strength is that I'm a really caring and non-judgemental person; and I know that this is essential when building a relationship with service users. I'm also very organised. This quality has really helped me in the past when it came to submitting and reviewing case reports, and planning activities. Finally, I'm an excellent communicator, who is not afraid of making big decisions. My communication skills help me to gain all of the information that is needed to make a final decision on particular cases. This is also useful for establishing a level of trust between myself and those I am working to help.'

4. What is your biggest weakness?

Be very careful when answering this question. You need to show a level of personal awareness, and strength of character. The worst thing you can say here is, 'I have none'. This will show a lack of sensitivity to the interviewer; and this could be particularly damning if you are applying for a role as a social worker. Try to select one weakness, which you believe working for the organisation will improve. Alternatively, select a weakness which you have already taken steps to improve, and show how you have done it. Make sure that the weakness you select is something that will not severely damage your ability to perform the role; the key is to show that you are someone who recognises their own limitations, and responds accordingly.

Sample response:

'My biggest weakness is that I have been known, at times, to put too much responsibility on myself. I'm someone who always wants to see a job done properly, and therefore I have a tendency to avoid delegating tasks to anyone else. This was particularly an issue at university. On one occasion I was placed in a team with three others. After two weeks, it became apparent that the other members of the team were discontented. This was because I had taken too much work, and not left them enough to do. We had a group meeting to resolve the issue and I quickly realised my mistake. I'm working extremely hard to fix this, as I know that working in a team is a vital requirement for any social worker.'

5. Why have you chosen social work as a career?

This is a really interesting question, and is your opportunity to show the employer how much you care about the role. It's a great chance for you to display your caring and compassionate nature, and show that you are serious about improving the lives of service users. If you really are someone who cares about industry, this should be an easy answer. You can even show some knowledge of public perceptions and media representations here.

Sample response:

'Social work is extremely important. I've always been interested in helping people, and for me the value of helping others to improve their lives surpasses any monetary gain. On a personal level, I have spent large portions of my childhood in contact with social workers who have changed my life for the better. I would not be where I am today without their support and guidance, and this has absolutely inspired me. Every time I read a negative media portrayal of the social sector, I think back to my own experiences; and how I want to help disprove the negative stereotypes associated with the role. This position really means something to me.'

6. **Describe a way in which you have resolved conflict in the social care workplace?**

This question is looking for you to demonstrate that you are someone who is capable of dealing with the type of issues commonly seen within the social sector. You should structure your response here, to make it as clear and concise as possible. Explain the issue, how you took action to resolve the issue, and the (positive) outcome of your methods.

Sample response:

'During my first year of university, I took a placement at a residential care home. I was required to support and assist the elderly residents with basic and personal tasks. On one occasion, I was sharing night shift duties with another junior assistant. I noticed that she was being abrasive and impatient whilst helping an elderly resident up the stairs. I took her to one side and explained how her behaviour was unacceptable, and needed to be improved. She accepted my criticism, apologised to the resident and following this made a conscious effort to change her approach. She is now employed full time at the care home, and is very popular with the residents.'

7. With the benefit of hindsight, is there anything you would do differently with one of your cases?

This is another really interesting question, which requires you to acknowledge that you can always improve upon your performance. The worst answer here is, 'no', as this demonstrates a lack of awareness. As a social worker, you should constantly be looking for ways to improve. When answering this question, take the same approach as in the previous. Talk about the issue, the steps you took to resolve the issue, and what you think you could have done differently. Remember that this question is referring specifically to one of your cases, so make sure that your example relates to someone you have dealt with personally.

Sample response:

'Whilst I was working at Ficshire Children's home, an incident oc-curred with a misbehaving child. As the senior manager was busy at the time, I was required to deal with the child myself. The child in question was a young boy, who had been driving his electronic race car around the living room of the house, despite being told on several occasions that he was not allowed to do this. I confiscated the toy, and he got very upset. Although my initial response was correct, I failed to communicate effectively with the boy as to why I was confis-cating the toy, and what was wrong with his behaviour. As a result, his behaviour got worse. As a social worker, I understand that mistakes will always be made; what is important is that we limit the damage of these mistakes, and do our utmost to improve whenever we can.'

8. **Can you describe a time when your actions made someone feel better?**

This is another situational based question, which requires you to draw on your past experience. As a social worker, it is imperative that you can reassure and support service users. If you have got to the point where you are being invited to interview for social work vacancies, then it is very likely you will have had experience of caring for or reassuring customers. Just as in the previous question, structure your response so that the interviewer gets a clear idea of what the issue was, how you acted to resolve the issue and what the outcome of your actions was.

Sample response:

'During my time working at Ficshire children's home, I was constantly in contact with vulnerable children. One such incident that I can remember, was when a little girl returned from a daytrip with potential foster parents. Whilst the foster parents seemed happy enough, the girl was very upset; and did not say goodbye to them upon returning to the house. I went up to speak to her, and discovered that she felt the foster parents did not like her. I found the contact details for her foster parents and gave them a call, to inform them of the situation. They were extremely surprised and immediately returned to the house, where they re-assured the girl that they had enjoyed the trip and wanted to do the same thing again. The girl was extremely happy about this, and a few months later, was officially fostered by the family.'

9. **When communicating with people, often verbal and non-verbal gestures can provide information. Give an example of how you have used your interpretation of either verbal or non-verbal behaviour, to help a service user?**

This is a difficult question, and one that requires you to display an advanced knowledge of body language and behavioural theory to answer. However, as with the previous question, if you have reached this point then it is unlikely that you will have an issue answering. Make sure you show the interviewer what the problem was, how you acted to resolve it and how the outcome was positive as a result of your actions. If you can bring in theoretical knowledge, then that will really improve your answer.

Sample response:

'When I was working in the student service team at my local primary school, a boy was brought into the office who had been misbehaving. The boy in question was very well known to the service team, as he had a history of truanting and skipping lessons. I interviewed him on a one-to-one basis, to try and get to the bottom of his behaviour. Upon discussion of his home life, it became apparent that his father had recently re-married. While he would not openly discuss this issue, he was extremely negative whenever he referred to his new step-mother. While he did not directly admit it, I decided that it was an avenue worth pursuing. We rang the boy's father, who came into the school and discussed the problems with his son. Steps were taken to improve the relationship between the child and his step-mother, and since then he has been behaving much better at school.'

10. Think of a client that you have disliked. How did you deal with this issue?

In this question, the asker wants you to demonstrate that you have the ability to provide the same service to all clients, regardless of how much you like them. This is really important. As a social worker, it would be impossible for you to get along with, or like every single person you meet. At some point you will inevitably come across people with whom you clash, or people who do not share the same values or morals as you. However, you must be able to put these feelings aside, and do what is right for the service user. Remember that you are there to help them, whether you like them or not.

Sample response:

'When I was working on the paediatric ward at my local hospital, I had to deal with a mother and father that I particularly disliked. The reason I disliked them was because they were extremely rude to the hospital staff, including myself, and treated us badly. They were impatient, demanding and constantly brought in their child for unnecessary checks. Eventually, we decided to have a meeting with the parents to voice our concerns. I was part of a team of 3 people who were assigned to communicate the issue. It became apparent that the parents were only acting out of concern for their child. While

they did not apologise for being rude, they did begin to visit with more reasonable frequency, and as such improved their relationship with the team. While I still did not particularly like them, because of their bad manners, I did my best to provide their child with the best possible treatment.'

11. What is your theoretical orientation?

This question is testing your knowledge of social theory and application. Theoretical orientation applies to the way in which you believe behaviour or personality can be explained. When answering this question, you should refer directly to theorists such as Freud, Pavlov and Maslow; and theories such as psycho-analytical, behavioural and humanistic. You probably won't be expected to produce an in-depth explanation of your chosen theory, the interviewer just wants to know that you have a good understanding of psychology and how you feel about the way people behave. Explain which theory you believe in, and give a brief explanation as to why.

onse:

'... ...ever in *Watson's behaviourist theory. The reason for this is that I feel as I have seen so many examples of times when behaviour has been learned through the environment that the individual has been placed in; and I firmly believe that behaviour can be observed, measured and consequently altered, to generate positive outcomes.'*

12. What types of clients do you have the most difficulty dealing with? Why do you think that is?

This question requires you to recognise that although you might try, you cannot deal with every single person with the same level of ease. Try to be honest, show that you are self-aware enough to recognise particular issues which still need to be overcome; and tell the organisation that you believe they are the best place to help you improve.

Sample response:

'I find working with alcoholism the most difficult. This is due to a family history of the problem; it's a very personal issue to me. When I worked at How2Helpp, I encountered several individuals with drink related issues. I did my absolute best to help these people in any way that I could, but it was still very upsetting. I'm working hard to improve myself, and I deliberately put myself in as many related situations as I could whilst at the organisation, to try and desensitise myself to the issue. While I would say that it still makes me feel uncomfortable, I am now more than happy to deal with it.'

As you can see, along with general interview questions, you are likely to be asked a large quantity of experience related questions. Using the college questions, university questions and all of the above, you should now have a great idea of what to expect from an interview. Below we have provided you with some top interview tips and tricks, to help you prepare for the day.

TOP INTERVIEW TIPS

- **Research the company.** Prior to the interview, make sure you have a good understanding of the company, their values, when they started, the services they offer, and the type of employees who work for them.

- **Practice.** Practice as many questions and answers as you possibly can. Write down sample responses to every question, read them aloud to yourself and practice on your friends and family. If you go through every potential question, there is no way you can be surprised by anything the interviewer asks. The more prepared you are, the more confidence you will exude, and the more likely you are to get the job.

- **Breath.** Whenever you are asked a question; lean back, take a deep breath and think about your answer. The interviewer will not judge you for carefully considering what to say. Another good trick is to ask the interviewer to repeat the question, to give you more time to think of a suitable answer.

- **Know your CV.** This is particularly true for interviews, such as social work, where you will be asked numerous experience based questions. It's really important that you have a strong knowledge of everything that you have put down in your resume, so that when you answer the questions, it matches with what is on the paper.

CHAPTER 9

A Day in the Life of a Social Worker

Once you have passed your interview, you will be offered a job. Your typical, everyday professional life will vary depending on the area in which you have chosen to specialise, and of course the organisation for whom you work. For example, if you are a social worker employed by the NHS, then you will have a vastly different experience to a social worker who is employed by their local authority. In this section of the book, we'll give you some examples of the kind of activities you might experience whilst working within the social sector. To do this, we'll run through a typical 'day in the life' of your average social worker.

BRIAN

Meet Brian. He is 35 years old, and is employed by his local authority as a child care social worker. Brian operates mainly from his office, but is often called upon to take field work and interact with families. Here is his typical day.

09:00

Brian arrives at his office at 09:00. He checks his diary for the day, and looks over specific case reports. At 10:00, Brian has a follow up, home visit appointment. After taking notes, drinking a coffee and making sure he has read through the case report thoroughly, Brian leaves for the appointment.

Brian's next case is as follows:

- The case surrounds a family of four, with a seven year old child and a new baby. The child, Kristopher, has not been attending school regularly.

- The house is being neglected and the mother, Kaylee, is struggling to deal with handling both Kristopher and her new baby.

- Brian has yet to meet Mr Johnson, the baby's father, but has been promised that he'll be present for today's meeting.

10:00

Brian arrives promptly at 10:00. He knocks on the door, several times, with no response. Eventually the door is answered by Kristopher. Kristopher enquires as to whether Brian is from the school, and seems delighted when he tells him that he is not. He directs Brian into the kitchen, which is extremely messy. The bins are overflowing and there are clothes strewn around the room. Kristopher's mother, Kaylee, is dealing with her baby. She avoids making eye contact with Brian. After Brian enquires as to why Kristopher is not at school, and is met with an unclear response, he sits down with Kaylee to discuss the situation. He is informed that Mr Johnson is 'out', this is deeply concerning for Brian.

Kaylee is confused as to why they need a visit from the social worker, but tells Brian that she is unable to make Kristopher go to school. At this point, Kristopher begins misbehaving. He runs around the room shouting and pulling faces; which produces an angry response from Kaylee. She sends him to his bedroom. After he has left, she complains to Brian that their GP won't provide medication for what she believes is 'hyperactive behaviour'. The baby is asleep in her cot, but appears well looked after and content. Brian tells Kaylee that he will be in touch later today.

11:00

After returning to his office, Brian discusses the case with his supervisor. They come to the conclusion that the best course of action would be to arrange a conference with all of the relevant support and welfare agencies involved with the case. This will help to agree a plan of action which will safeguard both of the children; and help Kaylee to cope better. Brian contacts the other agencies, and agrees a time and date. He then immediately calls Kaylee to let her know the decision, and to inform her of the time and date of the conference. She agrees to attend, and says that she will also bring along Mr. Johnson.

12:00

Brian's next task is to write up a 'young person's looked after review'. This concerns a boy named Kevin, who is transitioning to life with his new foster family, after a period in a children's home. Brian has worked with Kevin for over a year now, and he is extremely pleased with the boy's progression. Kevin is getting along great with his foster family, his grades are improving, and is no longer considered a risk. He is happy and positive about the future. Brian sends the report to his manager, and is pleased that he feels he's made a real difference to Kevin's life. He then looks over the case report for the next meeting.

The case is as follows:

- The case surrounds a father, Mr Hilliard, who is being assessed for sole custody of his daughter. His ex-partner is a heavy drinker and has acted irresponsibly in the past whilst taking care of his daughter.

- The father has previous sexual offences against children and has been noted, in the past, as being 'very controlling' towards his ex-partner.

13:00

At 13:00, Mr Hilliard arrives for his appointment. He is greeted by Brian and then taken into a separate room for an interview. This is Brian's first meeting with Mr Hilliard, and since he applied for sole custody, Mr Hilliard has not been assessed. Therefore it is Brian's role to perform an initial assessment, before follow up visits can be arranged with the relevant agencies to further inspect both his premises, and his suitability as a carer.

During the interview, Brian tries to gain an initial assessment of the following:

- Whether Mr Hilliard is liable to repeat his previous offences.

- Whether Mr Hilliard is applying for sole custody as a means of 'controlling' his ex- partner.

- Mr Hilliard's attitude towards his ex-partner.

- Mr Hilliard's current financial state, and any factors which he believes could hinder his ability to look after the child.

Brian comes away from the meeting with a less than positive impression of Mr Hilliard. He arranges a follow up visit, at the premises of Mr Hilliard, in 1 weeks' time.

14:00

Brian's next appointment involves visiting a young boy who has recently been placed in care. Both of his parents are alcoholics, and his father has been convicted on a charge of domestic abuse. His father is constantly in and out of prison, and has not been in contact with the boy for 2 weeks following his domestic abuse charge. The boy has not been informed of the circumstances and has been told that his father simply 'works far away.' Brian met with the mother last week, and discussed his intention to tell the boy the truth. The mother agreed that this was the best course of action, and today is the day that they will do it.

Upon arriving at the care home, and meeting with both the mother and boy, Brian invites them into an office to discuss the situation. The boy takes the news better than expected, but demands that he wants to visit his father in prison. While Brian does not feel this is the best idea, he is powerless to prevent it happening, and agrees to arrange a visit for the following week. After the meeting, Brian sits down with the manager of the care home to discuss the boy's recent progress, both at school and personally. He is currently underperforming educationally, and Brian arranges to contact the school to see whether special programmes can be put in place to help the boy improve.

15:00

Whilst he is on the way back to the office, Brian receives an extremely distressing phone call. It is from a colleague, who gives him the address of a girl who has reported that her father has purposefully burned her. Brian makes his way to the premises, and the door is answered by the girl. She is very distressed and begs Brian not to tell anybody. Her mother seems extremely disinterested, blames the girl and tells the child that if she doesn't like it, she should leave. The mother begins to get abusive and threatening with Brian, and he is eventually forced to call the police. A medical examination shows that the injury was deliberate; and the girl is immediately taken into care, with her mother and father both arrested. Brian spends the rest of the day and evening dealing with police enquiries, and consoling and calming the little girl.

While Brian is fortunate that he did not have any more field appointments, due to this unexpected incident, he is forced to backlog all of his paperwork until tomorrow. He finishes dealing with the incident at midnight, and gets home at 01:00.

KATHERINE

Our second social worker, Katherine, works as a senior member of a hospice social work team. This means that she works to provide emotional, social and practical support to patients and their friends and family. Let's have a look at her typical day.

08:30

At 08:30, Katherine arrives at the hospital. Her day starts at 09:00, but she gets there early to check her emails or any missed calls. Following this, she attends a meeting with her staff to discuss any referrals or issues from the previous day. One of the issues surrounds a man in the inpatient unit, who is struggling to come to terms with his terminal cancer diagnosis. Katherine has met with the man and his relatives before. While she is not surprised by this news, she is disappointed as she felt that he had been moving towards the stage of acceptance.

Following the meeting, Katherine goes to visit the man personally. She finds that he is extremely depressed and has not spoken to anyone in his family for several days. Katherine's immediate response is to try and counsel him, but this does not prove effective. As a senior member of the team, Katherine is heavily involved in the planning of the man's end of life wishes; with the aim of making him as comfortable and happy as possible. She eventually manages to persuade him to attend a meeting the following day, with some of his family, to try and discuss the issue further.

11:00

As part of Katherine's job, she also makes home visits to suffering patients. Her first visit of the day is an initial consultation with a woman who has been recently diagnosed with breast cancer. She was diagnosed 1 week ago, and has a child still in primary school. She is yet to discuss the diagnosis with her child, and is struggling with how to break the news. Katherine's role, initially, is to provide practical support. She discusses the different benefits that are available to the young woman, the type of home care that can be provided if she needs it and gives her contact details for various therapists whom she might find useful. Katherine arranges a follow up appointment for 1 week's time. The woman seems remarkably upbeat and positive. While this pleases Katherine, she knows that the woman faces an extremely difficult and emotional journey, and it is very possible that she'll be feeling differently the next time that Katherine sees her.

12:30

Katherine's next visit is to the home of a 75 year old man. The man has recently been told that there are no more treatment options available for his cancer. He has no wife and family, and is being visited once per day by his neighbour. The man refuses to move into a care home. Katherine's primary role today is to try and discuss his funeral arrangements; and again to persuade him to move into a care setting where his final weeks will be spent as comfortably as possible. The man again refuses to move into a care setting, but agrees to let Katherine help with the planning of his funeral. Katherine leaves this appointment feeling emotionally exhausted.

14:00

Following this, Katherine has a final home visit to the house of a 6 year old girl, who has been terminally diagnosed with brain cancer. Katherine is invited into the living room, where she meets several members of the girl's family. The aim of the meeting is to prepare a plan that will help grant the dying girl's final wishes, and make her last few weeks and months as painless and happy as possible. Both the family and the little girl appear to have come to terms with her diagnosis, and this is both an extremely painful and uplifting process for Katherine; as the group shares memories and plans ahead of the final few weeks. One of the aims of the family is to take the little girl to Disney Land, before she passes. Katherine promises to do all she can to assist them with this endeavour, and arranges a follow up appointment at the hospice between just the girl, her mother and father for next week.

15:30

When she gets back to her office, Katherine spends the rest of the afternoon responding to emails and phone calls, and planning a training programme which she is aiming to facilitate in both her own hospice; and in others. She is preparing a presentation to highlight the methods of the training programme; which will improve staff-patient relationships and communication, in relation to discussing terminal illness.

18:00

Katherine looks over her schedule for tomorrow, visits several inpatients individually to discuss their circumstances, and then goes home.

GEORGIA

Georgia is our third and final social worker. She is the lead social worker at a school, and aims to provide support to students, teachers and student services. Let's have a look at her typical day.

07:30

Georgia arrives at work at 7:30. As a school social worker, her day corresponds with the opening hours of the school; therefore she starts earlier than the majority of other social workers. She immediately goes to her office and runs through her scheduled appointments and case reports for the day. After visiting the staff room, her first appointment begins at 09:00.

09:00

At 09:00, Georgia meets with a 15 year old student from year 11. The boy in question is extremely depressed and won't speak to anyone. From studying her case reports, Georgia establishes that the reason for this behaviour is because the boy has recently split up from his girlfriend. He is skipping lessons, and has been threatening to take his own life.

Since he is refusing to communicate, Georgia comes up with a novel idea to help him express himself. She gives him a pen and paper and encourages him to write down his thoughts and feelings, instead of verbalising them. The boy is initially hesitant, but eventually complies. He writes for ten minutes, before passing the paper back over to Georgia. She reads through it, verbalises her thoughts and then gives him back the paper to write again. This goes on for half an hour; and through this method of communication, Georgia is able to establish why the boy is feeling the way he is, why he wants to take his own life, why he doesn't want to talk to people and why he has begun skipping lessons. She is extremely concerned about the boy, and after he leaves, gives his parents a call. They confess to knowing about the problem; but are unsure of what to do. Georgia arranges a follow up appointment with all three of them, and refers them to various therapists who she feels could help the issue.

Following this, Georgia visits the student services team and encourages that the school pay for counselling sessions which could help alleviate the boy's problems. A programme of 4 to 5 sessions is subsequently arranged with a local counsellor.

10:00

At 10:00, Georgia has a meeting with one of the teaching staff, to discuss a particular student in his form. This is a follow up to a previous appointment, where a detailed behavioural plan was drawn up. The boy in question has been aggressive towards both teachers and other pupils, acting out in lessons, refusing to take part in class discussions and generally misbehaving. After 3 weeks implementation of the behavioural plan, the student's behaviour has not changed at all. Therefore, Georgia and the teacher draw up a 'Plan B', which also involves the student's parents. Georgia arranges to speak to the boy later in the day.

11:00

At 11:00, Georgia makes a home visit to one of the pupils, Amanda. Amanda is 15 years old, and has a previous history of putting herself in sexually threatening situations. She lives with her single mother, and is aggressive and abusive towards her. Amanda has been known to punch and kick her mother when she loses her temper; and her grades at school are extremely poor.

Georgia has been overseeing home mediation lessons between the two, in order to try and improve relations and positively affect Amanda's marks. These have been getting steadily better over the last few weeks, but when she arrives at the home today; she finds her mother crying. She claims that her daughter punched her in the stomach and then left the house. Georgia spends an hour consoling and chatting with the mother, arranges a follow up for next week and promises that she will meet with Amanda if she sees her at school. In order to make sure of this, she immediately calls student services to tell the staff to detain her if she is found on the school premises. On the way back to the school, she gets a call saying that Amanda is now in the student services office.

12:30

At 12:30, Georgia arrives back at the school. She immediately goes to the student services office, where she picks up Amanda. She was caught smoking outside of the school gates, and is very unhappy to see Georgia. The student service team claim that she won't communicate with them and is largely unrepentant about her behaviour. Georgia takes her into a room and tries to negotiate with her, to get her side of the story. Amanda refuses to speak to Georgia, and in a show of defiance, flicks cigarette ash in her face. Georgia tries to remain calm, and continues her attempts at negotiation. Amanda still refuses to co-operate, and gets continually more abusive towards Georgia. Eventually she is forced to call student services to take her away. Georgia rings Amanda's mother to inform her of the situation, and gives her a personal number which she can use to contact her at any time. Amanda's mother is extremely grateful for this.

13:45

At 13:45, Georgia meets with the boy who is having behavioural problems, from earlier in the day. His name is Paul. This is not the first time they have met, and Paul has always been quite open about his own behaviour when speaking to her. Today is no different, but Georgia takes a firmer approach; due to the fact that Paul agreed with but did not demonstrate the proposed changes in behaviour. By all accounts, Paul has a relatively happy home life and is well looked after by his friends and family. Georgia attempts to demonstrate the downsides of his behaviour, and makes him promise to agree to another behavioural plan, which will have harsher consequences if he does not comply.

14:30

At 14:30, Georgia has a joint meeting with the two heads of student services, and a misbehaving pupil. The pupil in question is named Jessica, and she has just been removed from her art lesson after she threw an inkpot at the teachers head. The aim of the meeting is to get to the bottom of her behaviour and establish a suitable course of punishment. Jessica seems fairly repentant, although she maintains that the teacher in question was abusive towards her. Jessica has a history of bad behaviour; and this is not the first time she has been involved with student services. Between them, Georgia and the student services manage to convince her to participate in a one-to-one meeting with her art teacher, so that the two can try to understand each other better.

15:15

As the day is finishing, Georgia goes through her case reports, makes written assessments and prepares her schedule for the next day. She also gives Amanda's mother a call, to see how she is doing; and promises that she is always there if she needs help. All of this takes approximately an hour and a half to complete, and Georgia returns home at 17:00.

As you can see from the three sample days that we have provided you, as a social worker you should be prepared for anything. You never know how a service user might respond to a certain situation or problem; and you must be equipped to deal with any emotional reaction or response. You will be required to think on your feet, show empathy, compassion and understanding; and be prepared to work extra hours to ensure that every one of your clients are comfortable and secure. You'll face some extremely difficult situations, but the opportunity to change people's lives for the better, makes it all worthwhile.

CHAPTER 10

A few final words
& useful links

You have now reached the end of our guide, and will no doubt be more prepared than you were at the start of the book. There are a huge number of different options available for aspiring social workers, but whichever option you take, be confident in the knowledge that you can make a real difference to people's lives. Social work is extremely difficult, and the emotional challenges that it brings are certainly not for everyone.

We really hope that reading this book has given you a wider scope of the situations you are likely to encounter. Social work is hard, but it's also incredibly interesting. No two situations are the same, every person that you work with will provide fresh challenges and difficulties to overcome. Remember that your most powerful tool is yourself. If you are truly a caring, empathetic and understanding person; then there is nobody that you can't help if you set your mind to it. Believe in the power of positive change, and you will be a fantastic asset to any social work team.

Before you close this guide, and begin your career as a social worker, here are a few things to consider:

- Gain as much practical experience as you can, as early as you can, through voluntary organisations.

- Remember to treat every service user with the same level of kindness, politeness and understanding, regardless of their situation or how much you like them.

- Be prepared for challenging and emotional situations, which will test you to your very limits. With the right experience and knowledge, you can go into any one of these situations confident of doing your best.

- Stay organised. Organisation is key for a good social worker. You need to have your own affairs in order, to help other people manage theirs.

USEFUL LINKS

Health and Care Professions Council, HCPC. http://www.hpc-uk.org/

British Association of Social Workers, BASW. https://www.basw.co.uk/

The College of Social Work, http://www.tcsw.org.uk/home/

CSV Voluntary Organisation, http://www.csv.org.uk

Frontline http://thefrontline.org.uk

Step Up http://www.stepuptosocialwork.co.uk

British Association of Social Workers https://www.basw.co.uk/

NVCO Volunteer Centres https://www.ncvo.org.uk/ncvo-volunteering

Bury College
Millennium LRC